MASTER THE ART OF WOK COOKING

THE GOLDEN WOK

DIANA CHAN

MASTER THE
ART OF WOK
COOKING

THE
GOLDEN
WOK

Hardie Grant

BOOKS

DIANA
CHAN

WOK BASICS
10

SAUCES & MORE
20

MEAT & POULTRY
114

SEAFOOD
138

SNACKS
42

NOODLES & RICE
74

VEGETABLES
182

INTRODUCTION

The smell of a wok heating over an open flame reminds me of home, Johor Bahru in Malaysia. It is where my parents live, and where I spent most of my childhood. Johor Bahru is a working-class town, and there isn't much to do there unless you are a local. One of the upsides, though, is that it's just across the border with Singapore. So, when I was young, my two older siblings, our parents and I would frequent Singapore almost every weekend to eat and explore.

During the week, my mum would often return home after a long day at work, fire up the wok and cook char bee hoon – a dish made from fried vermicelli noodles, flavoured with pork neck or belly, prawns, bean sprouts and egg. My job was to pick the tails off the bean sprouts. It was tedious and time-consuming, but made me appreciate the finer details that go into preparing a dish, even if it's just a simple, home-cooked meal.

My mum, Molly, is a meticulous cook and takes pride in her Peranakan lineage. Many of the dishes she makes have been passed down to her through generations, and I am still in the process of learning them. She cooks according to taste and feel. She relies on her senses rather than referring to written recipes, so the only way I can learn is to watch her and taste as she cooks.

My dad, Joe, is an excellent cook too, but is the complete opposite of Mum. His cooking style is quick and simple – I call him the barbecue master! I don't know anyone who can cook seafood on the barbie better than Dad; it's always perfect.

Depending on the heritage of the household, char bee hoon can be known by a different name, but we've always called it char bee hoon because Mum is of Hokkien descent. The noodle dish is kind of like an Asian one-pot wonder and takes no time at all to prepare. The same can be said for almost every dish that is made in a wok.

Cooking with a wok is a way of life throughout Asia. Many people think a wok is used exclusively for stir-frying, but a wok is the most versatile and inexpensive piece of kitchen equipment you can own. It can be used for shallow- and deep-frying, steaming, boiling, braising and smoking.

A wok was among the first things I bought when I relocated to Melbourne at age nineteen. Although I always felt welcome in Australia, I missed Malaysia a lot when I initially moved. I missed my family and friends, and I really missed the food. It was hard to find good South-East Asian food at that time, which is certainly not the case these days. While I was busy studying accounting, I would find comfort in the kitchen and make meals that reminded me of home and my parents' cooking. Looking back now, sending me to Melbourne for university was the best decision my mum and dad could've made for me.

In 2017, my life changed when I won *MasterChef Australia*. It was a surreal, but incredibly rewarding experience that has opened up so many different doors and presented so many opportunities for me to be able to pursue a career in food. Since then, I have run a pop-up Malaysian street-food restaurant called Chanteen; hosted various cooking shows, including my own show, *Asia Unplated*; developed a range of dumplings, which are available in major supermarkets; worked with tourism boards; and appeared as a guest chef at festivals and events in lots of different countries. I feel so lucky that I am able to travel for work. Seeing the world and learning about different cultures and cuisines has always been a passion of mine. It's also eye-opening to work with chefs from different walks of life.

When I am at home in Melbourne, I visit the Prahran and South Melbourne markets almost every day to buy fresh produce. In addition to creativity, the thing I love most about cooking is the enjoyment I get when I feed people, especially my friends and loved ones. My partner, Hugh, and I host dinner parties in our home at least once a week. A typical meal at our place features a plethora of generous, share-style dishes laid on the table for everyone to help themselves.

The food is often themed too, so it could be Italian, Indian or Chinese one week, then Japanese or Peranakan the next. It all depends on how much time I have to prepare the meal. If I don't have a lot of it, I'll fire up the wok and cook one, or more, of the recipes that feature in this cookbook. They work just as well for dinner parties as they do for midweek meals, trust me!

They're quick, fresh and smoky – everything a great wok-made dish should be.

01

WOK
BASICS

It's no surprise that you'll need a wok to cook the recipes in this book. So, how do you choose the best one for you? It all depends on your cooking preferences and the type of stove you have. In this chapter, I'll walk you through the most common types of woks and their characteristics, tips on how to care for your wok so it lasts a lifetime, plus some important techniques to help you master the art of wok cooking.

Woks can be made from different materials, and although they're essentially designed to work in the same way, they all produce slightly different results.

CARBON STEEL

Carbon steel woks are the most traditional and popular choice for many home cooks and professional chefs. They heat up quickly and distribute heat evenly, making them ideal for stir-frying. They also develop a natural non-stick surface over time, enhancing their cooking performance. However, they require regular seasoning and proper care to prevent rusting.

CAST IRON

Cast iron woks are known for their excellent heat retention and even heat distribution. They are highly durable and can last for generations. Like carbon steel woks, they require seasoning to maintain their non-stick surface. The only downside is their weight. They usually come with handles on either side but are heavy, so aren't as easy to move around as woks with a single timber handle.

NON-STICK

Non-stick woks have a non-stick coating that makes them convenient for cooking without food sticking to the surface. They are easy to clean and don't require seasoning. However, they cannot reach the same high heat as traditional woks and your dishes may not develop the same flavour.

STAINLESS STEEL

Stainless steel woks are durable and do not require seasoning. They are resistant to rust and staining, making them low-maintenance. However, they do not heat as evenly as carbon steel or cast iron, and may not provide the same level of high-heat cooking.

Once you've chosen which wok suits you, the best place to start looking for one is at your local Asian supermarket. If you buy a good-quality wok and season it properly, I can guarantee it will be your new favourite kitchen item, and it will even improve as it gets older.

FLAT BASE VS ROUND BASE

The type of wok you choose will ultimately be determined by the stove you have. The most traditional wok set-up would be a cast iron wok over a charcoal burner, but very few of us have the space, time or patience to heat up coals.

If you own a stove with a level cooking surface, such as an electric stove or induction cooktop, you will need to purchase a flat-based wok. If you own a gas stove or wok burner, you can use either a flat- or round-based wok. However, I would highly recommend opting for the round base. It will give you a better result every time, as the area of intense heat is more concentrated. You will need to ensure the wok sits as close to the heat source as possible. If you find the wok is unstable, you may require a wok ring to help hold it in place.

SIZE MATTERS

The size of a wok is also very important. If you are a beginner, I would suggest you choose one that is fairly light and easy to handle, so you can first master the techniques.

Personally, I prefer a large wok – one that is 36 cm (14¼ in) or 40 cm (15¾ in) in diameter. This is because when you cook in a wok you tend to toss food around. Wok cooking is all about speed and applying maximum heat so your food will cook quickly. You need the space to do this. Another bonus of using a large wok is that you get to use it for other cooking methods, such as steaming whole fish, deep-frying or boiling.

HOW TO SEASON A WOK

It is imperative to season a carbon steel or cast iron wok to create a natural non-stick surface. Here is my simple, step-by-step guide.

1. Wash the wok in warm, soapy water, scrubbing lightly to remove any preservative coating that has been applied at the factory. Rinse well, drain excess water, then place the wok over a low heat to dry.

2. Add a little neutral-flavoured cooking oil, such as vegetable or peanut oil, then use a paper towel to coat the surface of the wok evenly with the oil. Be careful not to burn yourself. Heat gently for 10–15 minutes, then wipe off the oil with a clean paper towel. The paper towel should look black after this step; don't be alarmed, this is natural.

3. Continue wiping until the paper towel comes away clean. The wok will darken as you go.

4. Add in a little more oil along with some aromatics, such as spring onion, garlic and ginger (peeled and roughly chopped), and stir-fry until fragrant. The wok will adopt the flavours of the aromatics. Remove and discard the aromatics. Once cool, wipe down the wok and it is ready to use.

HOW TO CLEAN A WOK

A properly seasoned carbon steel or cast iron wok should not be washed with soap. First, remove any food that has stuck to its surface. While the wok is still warm, use a soft brush or sponge and wash the wok in hot water only. Place the wok over a low heat for a few minutes to dry any water droplets. Leave to cool, then coat with a little oil.

If your wok is made of a non-stick material or stainless steel, clean the wok as you would any other cookware.

Note: If a wok isn't seasoned or stored in a dry place, it may develop rust. If this happens, rub it down with steel wool then season it again. A cast iron or carbon steel wok is less likely to rust if it is lightly oiled before being stored. Highly acidic or alkaline foods can also degrade the wok's seasoning.

ESSENTIAL TOOLS AND ACCESSORIES

WOK SPATULA

A wok spatula has a long handle and a flat, slightly curved edge. It's specifically designed for stir-frying and flipping food in a wok. It's essential for maneuvering ingredients around the curved surface.

LADLE

A ladle is useful for spooning liquids out of a wok. I recommend choosing one that has a deep bowl. Some ladles even have graduated markings inside that indicate how much liquid they hold, which can be handy if you're following a recipe or need to know specific measurements.

LONG CHOPSTICKS OR TONGS

Long chopsticks or tongs are great for flipping and stirring food in a wok. They provide more dexterity than the wok spatula and are the best tools for delicate ingredients.

WOK SKIMMER OR STRAINER

A wok skimmer, also known as a wok strainer, is typically made of metal or bamboo and features a long handle and a wide, flat, perforated or mesh-like scoop at the end. It is particularly useful for deep-frying, blanching or removing boiled ingredients from a wok.

Note: If using a non-stick wok, choose utensils made from softer materials, such as timber, bamboo or silicone, to avoid damaging the wok's surface.

DOMED LID

If you are planning to use your wok as a steamer, then I highly recommend getting a domed lid that fits snugly. The domed shape means any condensation will run down the sides rather than the middle, so water doesn't end up in your dish. The lid will also come in handy for stir-frying if you wish to achieve less char.

COOKING TIPS AND TECHNIQUES

STIR-FRYING

— It is essential to preheat the wok first. Once it is hot, use a squeeze bottle to apply oil to the inner rim of the wok so that it coats the surface evenly.

— Don't overcrowd the wok. If you're cooking for a large group of people, you can stir-fry ingredients in batches, so the wok retains its heat.

— To ensure even cooking, always add the ingredients that take a long time to cook first, such as firm root vegetables.

DEEP-FRYING

— Ensure the wok is stable before filling it with oil. Use a wok ring, if required.

— Always add cold oil to a cold wok, then slowly bring it up to temperature.

— Never fill a wok more than one-third full with oil.

— If the oil catches fire, turn off the heat (if you can) and cover the wok with a metal lid or large baking tray. This will cut off the oxygen supply and the fire will extinguish. Never throw water on an oil fire and do not try to move the wok as the hot oil may spill.

— For most ingredients, the oil temperature should reach 170–180°C/340–360°F. You can use an oil thermometer or test the temperature with a wooden chopstick. If you see tiny bubbles gather around it, the oil is hot enough. (Alternatively, use a cube of bread. If it turns golden in 45 seconds, the oil is ready. Any quicker and the oil is too hot.)

— Don't overcrowd the wok. Fry in batches and allow the oil to return to an optimal temperature before adding the next batch.

STEAMING & BOILING

— Ensure the wok is stable before filling it with water. Use a wok ring, if required.

— During steaming, check the water level and top up, if necessary.

— Always open the lid away from you using a towel or oven mitt, so the steam doesn't scald your face or skin.

MEASUREMENTS

— Please note, this book uses 15 ml (½ fl oz) tablespoons.

WHAT IS WOK HEI?

Wok hei is a Cantonese term, which translates to 'breath of the wok'. It describes a distinctive flavour and aroma that is achieved when stir-frying in a wok at very high temperatures. The more you cook in the wok, the more flavour it will impart.

A NOTE ON PREPARATION

Successful wok cooking is all about preparation, especially when you are stir-frying. It is essential to prepare all the ingredients before you turn the stove on. That way, everything is sliced, diced and ready to be added to the wok at a moment's notice, because there will be no time to run to the pantry or fridge mid-cook.

02

SAUCES & MORE

CHILLI CRAB

An iconic sauce made popular by the Singapore chilli crab. Just make sure you have enough steamed or fried buns to mop up all the goodness!

MAKES 1 litre (34 fl oz/4 cups)
PREPARATION TIME 15 minutes
COOKING TIME 25 minutes

125 ml (4 fl oz/½ cup) neutral-flavoured cooking oil

4 teaspoons fermented soybean paste (taucu)

200 g (7 oz) tomato passata (puréed tomatoes)

125 g (4½ oz/½ cup) tomato sauce (ketchup)

2 tablespoons rice vinegar

3 tablespoons caster (superfine) sugar

2 teaspoons cornflour (cornstarch) mixed into a slurry with 2 tablespoons water

1 × 70 g (2½ oz) egg

SPICE PASTE

70 g (2½ oz) long red chillies, chopped

100 g (3½ oz) spring onions (scallions)

30 g (1 oz) garlic

10 g (¼ oz) piece fresh ginger, sliced

10 g (¼ oz) piece fresh galangal, sliced

20 g (¾ oz) lemongrass stem, white part only, chopped

4 teaspoons belacan (shrimp paste), toasted (see tip on page 97)

30 g (1 oz) dried baby shrimp, rehydrated in warm water for at least 15 minutes and drained

Start by preparing the spice paste. Place all the spice paste ingredients in a high-speed blender and blend until smooth.

Heat the wok over a medium heat then add the oil. Fry the spice paste until fragrant, for about 5 minutes.

Add the soybean paste, passata, tomato sauce, vinegar, sugar and 500 ml (17 fl oz/2 cups) water. Allow to simmer for 10–15 minutes.

Once the mixture has thickened slightly, add the cornflour slurry. Allow to thicken further over low heat before cracking in the egg and swirling it into the sauce to create ribbons.

Tips: This sauce is used for chilli crabs, or you can use it for other seafood, such as prawns or squid. Store in a clean, sterile, airtight container in the refrigerator for up to 1 week.

BLACK PEPPER

This is a classic sauce that is versatile and pairs beautifully with seafood. There's a lovely balance between sweet and salty flavours in this sauce as well as a hint of chilli and fragrant fried curry leaves.

MAKES 500 ml (17 fl oz/2 cups)
PREPARATION TIME 15 minutes
COOKING TIME 15 minutes

2 tablespoons neutral-flavoured cooking oil

20 g (¾ oz) black peppercorns, toasted and ground into a coarse powder

20 g (¾ oz) piece fresh ginger, julienned

50 g (1¾ oz) spring onions (scallions), finely chopped

20 g (¾ oz) garlic, crushed

10 g (¼ oz) curry leaves

10 g (¼ oz) long red chillies, finely sliced

10 g (¼ oz) dried bird's eye chillies

2 teaspoons white sugar

2 tablespoons oyster sauce

1 tablespoon soy sauce

1 tablespoon dark cooking caramel (substitute with kecap manis)

Heat the wok over a high heat then add the oil. Fry the peppercorns for 30 seconds, until fragrant.

Add the ginger, spring onions, garlic, curry leaves and all the chillies. Fry for 1–2 minutes, until fragrant.

Add the sugar, sauces and caramel and stir through to combine.

Tip: Store in a clean, sterile, airtight container in the refrigerator for up to 4 weeks.

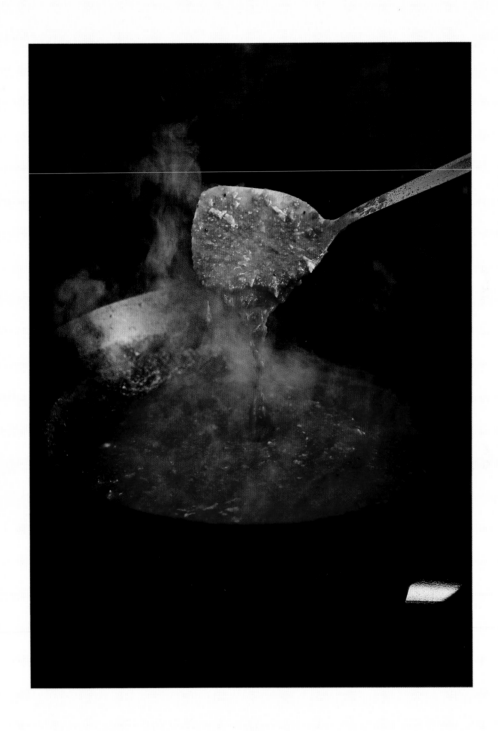

SAMBAL BALADO

Red chilli sambal

Sambal balado is a highly versatile condiment popular in Indonesia. It is made with chillies and tomatoes that have been cooked down to a relish. Add extra flavour to your protein by serving it with meat, fish, poultry or eggs.

MAKES   300 g (10½ oz)
PREPARATION TIME   10 minutes (+ cooling)
COOKING TIME   18 minutes

100 g (3½ oz)
red Asian shallots,
chopped

50 g (1¾ oz) tomato
(roma or gourmet),
chopped

300 g (10½ oz) long
red chillies, seeded
and chopped

60 ml (2 fl oz/¼ cup)
neutral-flavoured
cooking oil

2 teaspoons white
sugar, plus extra
to taste

1 teaspoon salt, plus
extra to taste

2 tablespoons lime
juice

Blitz the shallots and tomato in a food processor for 5 seconds, then add the chillies and process until a coarse paste forms.

Heat a wok over a low–medium heat then add the oil. Cook the shallot paste, sugar and salt, stirring occasionally, for 10–15 minutes until thickened and deep red in colour, but not browned. Stir in the lime juice, then adjust with extra sugar or salt, if necessary. Transfer to a bowl and set aside to cool.

Tip: Store in a clean, sterile, airtight container in the refrigerator for up to 6 weeks.

CHILLI VINEGAR SAUCE

MAKES 150 ml (5 fl oz)
PREPARATION TIME 5 minutes

30 g (1 oz) garlic

30 g (1 oz) red Thai chillies

pinch of salt

80 ml (2½ fl oz/ ⅓ cup) white vinegar

1 teaspoon caster (superfine) sugar

This condiment can be paired with many dishes, such as chicken rice, fried oyster omelette or steamed prawns. A good chilli vinegar sauce is often heavy on the garlic with a good spicy hit and a slight sweetness to it.

Mash the garlic, chillies and salt in a mortar with a pestle until a smooth paste forms.

Add the vinegar and sugar. Mix well then serve.

Tip: Store in a clean, sterile, airtight container in the refrigerator for up to 1 week.

FIVE-SPICE POWDER

MAKES 180 g (6½ oz)
PREPARATION TIME 5 minutes
COOKING TIME 5 minutes

30 g (1 oz) cinnamon stick, broken

30 g (1 oz) cloves

60 g (2 oz) fennel seeds

30 g (1 oz) sichuan peppercorns

30 g (1 oz) star anise

The holy grail of spice mixes in Chinese cooking, five-spice powder is used to flavour meats and added to marinades and sauces. A good one to keep in your repertoire!

Dry-roast all the spices in a wok over low heat until fragrant.

Transfer the spices to a spice grinder and blend into a fine powder. (Alternatively, use a mortar and pestle.)

Tip: Store in a clean, sterile, airtight container or jar in a cool, dark place for up to 24 months.

SAUCES & MORE

FRIED SHALLOTS *AND* SHALLOT OIL

You can't go wrong with having a large batch of fried shallots and shallot oil on hand. They are packed full of flavour and add a whole new dimension to a dish in terms of aroma and texture.

MAKES 100 g (3½ oz) fried shallots and 200 ml (7 fl oz) shallot oil
PREPARATION TIME 30 minutes (+ 10 minutes cooling)
COOKING TIME 15 minutes

450 g (1 lb) red Asian shallots

480 ml (16¼ fl oz) neutral-flavoured cooking oil

Peel the shallots and thinly slice crossways.

Heat a wok over a low–medium heat then add the oil. Drop a slice of shallot into the oil to test if it is sufficiently hot. If it is, add all the shallots. Stir gently to brown evenly, for about 10–15 minutes.

As soon as the shallots are a light brown colour, transfer them from the hot oil to a metal strainer. The shallots will continue to brown to a golden colour.

When the oil is cool enough to handle, strain it into a clean, sterile, airtight jar.

Allow fried shallots to cool completely before transferring them to clean, sterile, airtight jars.

Tip: Store in a cool, dark place and use within 1 month.

XO SAUCE

This sauce can be added to rice dishes such as any fried rice, sprinkled over as a topping for noodles or used to amp up your vegetable dishes. The options for this incredibly versatile sauce are endless!

MAKES 1 kg (2 lb 3 oz)
PREPARATION TIME 30 minutes
(+ 2 hours soaking)
COOKING TIME 30 minutes

300 g (10½ oz)
dried scallops

300 g (10½ oz)
dried baby shrimp

200 g (7 oz) Jinhua
ham (substitute with
prosciutto or speck)

300 g (10½ oz)
red Asian shallots

150 g (5¼ oz) garlic

20 g (¾ oz) bird's
eye chillies

1 litre (34 fl oz/
4 cups) neutral-
flavoured cooking oil

60 ml (2 fl oz/
¼ cup) XO brandy
(substitute with any
shaoxing rice wine
or sherry)

400 ml (13½ fl oz)
chicken stock

4 teaspoons soft
brown sugar

1 tablespoon oyster
sauce

2 tablespoons dark
mushroom soy sauce

80 ml (2½ fl oz/
⅓ cup) fish sauce

2 tablespoons chilli
flakes

Start by rehydrating the dried seafood. In two separate bowls, cover the scallops and shrimp with hot water and soak for at least 2 hours.

Meanwhile, finely dice the ham and shallots. Crush the garlic. Remove the seeds from the bird's eye chillies and finely dice.

When the dried seafood has softened, drain and blend separately in a food processor until coarsely chopped. (You still want a little bit of texture.)

Heat the oil to 100°C (210°F) in a wok over a medium heat. Fry the scallops for 3–5 minutes. Add the shrimp and fry for a further 5–7 minutes. Add the ham and bird's eye chillies and fry for another 5–7 minutes until the seafood and ham are crispy.

Using a slotted spoon, transfer the seafood mixture to a bowl. Return the wok to medium heat and fry the shallots and garlic for 3 minutes.

Deglaze the wok with the brandy. Allow it to evaporate slightly then add the stock, sugar, oyster sauce and mushroom sauce. Simmer until half of the liquid has evaporated.

When the liquid has cooked off, carefully pour the seafood mixture back into the wok. Adjust the heat to low and stir to combine. Add the fish sauce and chilli flakes and stir to combine.

Transfer to clean, sterile, airtight containers, and set aside to cool on the counter before refrigerating. The sauce can be stored for up to 3 months.

Tips: You can eat the XO sauce right away or let the flavours meld for 2–3 days before digging in.

SAMBAL HAE BEE

Shrimp sambal

This condiment is not for the faint-hearted. It is strong and pungent in both smell and flavour but it is such a beauty when eaten with white bread or rice.

MAKES 300 g (10½ oz/2 cups)
PREPARATION TIME 30 minutes
COOKING TIME 20 minutes

200 g (7 oz) dried baby shrimp, rehydrated in warm water for 30 minutes and drained

neutral-flavoured cooking oil, for frying

40 g (1½ oz) tamarind purée

40 g (1½ oz) white sugar

10 g (¼ oz) makrut lime leaves, thinly sliced, reserving some for garnish

salt, to taste

SPICE PASTE

10 g (¼ oz) dried red chillies, seeded, rehydrated in warm water for at least 15 minutes and drained

30 g (1 oz) long red chillies, seeded and roughly chopped

100 g (3½ oz) red Asian shallots, roughly chopped

30 g (1 oz) garlic

4 teaspoons belacan (shrimp paste), toasted (see tip on page 97)

30 g (1 oz) piece fresh galangal, sliced

50 g (1¾ oz) lemongrass stem, white part only, chopped

10 g (¼ oz) piece fresh turmeric, sliced

1 tablespoon neutral-flavoured cooking oil

Drain the rehydrated shrimp and pulse in a food processor until coarsely chopped. Set aside.

To make the spice paste, blend all the spice paste ingredients in a high-speed blender until smooth.

Heat a wok over a high heat then add the oil. Fry the spice paste until fragrant – this should take 3–5 minutes.

Add the shrimp and stir through until the mixture has dried out – this should take around 10–12 minutes. (You are looking for a semi-dry mixture.)

Add the tamarind and sugar and season with salt. Add the lime leaves and stir for 2 minutes. Remove from the heat.

Serve with rice or as I like mine: with some butter on fresh white bread.

Tip: Store in a clean, sterile, airtight container in the refrigerator for up to 1 month.

SAUCES & MORE

SAMBAL TUMIS

Dried chilli sambal

MAKES 250 g (9 oz)
PREPARATION TIME 10 minutes
COOKING TIME 15 minutes

125 ml (4 fl oz/ ½ cup) neutral-flavoured cooking oil

100 g (3½ oz) red Asian shallots, thinly sliced

100 g (3½ oz) dried chilli paste (chilli boh)

40 g (1½ oz / ¼ cup) grated palm sugar (jaggery)

4 teaspoons tamarind purée

pinch of salt

I can't emphasise how much use you will get out of this condiment. You can use it to flavour absolutely anything and it's even great on its own.

Heat a wok over a medium heat then add the oil. Fry the shallots until softened. Add the chilli paste and toss to combine.

Add the palm sugar, tamarind and 125 ml (4 fl oz/½ cup) water and cook until the sugar has dissolved. Season with the salt.

Tip: Store in a clean, sterile, airtight container in the refrigerator for up to 3 weeks.

SAMBAL HIJAU

Green sambal

MAKES 350 g (12½ oz)
PREPARATION TIME 15 minutes
COOKING TIME 15 minutes

300 g (10½ oz) large green chillies, chopped

20 g (¾ oz) green bird's eye chillies, chopped

100 g (3½ oz) red Asian shallots, chopped

200 g (7 oz) green tomatoes, chopped

2 tablespoons neutral-flavoured cooking oil

50 g (1¾ oz) lemongrass stem, white part only, bruised

5 g (⅛ oz) makrut lime leaves, torn

½ lime, zested and juiced

20 g (¾ oz) white sugar, plus extra to taste

1 teaspoon salt, plus extra to taste

This sambal has a slight herbaceous quality. It is vibrant and green and slightly tart in flavour from the green tomatoes. It is a great alternative to its sister sambal balado, which is red and fiery.

Blitz the chillies, shallots and tomatoes in a food processor until a coarse paste forms.

Heat a wok over a low–medium heat then add the oil. Cook the chilli paste, lemongrass and lime leaves for 5 minutes, stirring regularly.

Stir in the lime zest and juice, sugar and salt and cook for a further 10 minutes or until the liquid has evaporated. Remove and discard the lemongrass and lime leaves, then adjust with more sugar or salt to taste, if necessary.

Tip: Store in a clean, sterile, airtight container in the refrigerator for up to 4 weeks.

SAMBAL KICAP

*Sweet and salty
soy dipping sauce*

MAKES 250 g (9 oz)
PREPARATION TIME 5 minutes
COOKING TIME 15 minutes

125 ml (4 fl oz/
½ cup) neutral-
flavoured cooking oil

30 g (1 oz) bird's
eye chillies, stalks
removed

30 g (1 oz) red Asian
shallots, roughly
chopped

30 g (1 oz) garlic

175 ml (6 fl oz)
kecap manis

salt, to taste

This is a popular sweet and salty dipping sauce that can be served with grilled fish or meat, mee soto (spicy noodle soup) and even banana fritters.

Place a wok over a medium-high heat then add the oil. Add the chillies, shallots and garlic and fry for 5 minutes.

Remove from the heat and transfer the mixture to a high-speed blender. Blend until a coarse paste forms. Add the kecap manis and season with salt.

Tip: Store in a clean, sterile, airtight container in the refrigerator for up to 1 week.

SAMBAL BELACAN

Shrimp paste sambal

MAKES 100 g (3½ oz)
PREPARATION TIME 5 minutes

60 g (2 oz) long red
chillies, seeded and
chopped

20 g (¾ oz) bird's
eye chillies, seeded
and chopped

2 tablespoons
belacan (shrimp
paste), toasted (see
tip on page 97)

2 calamansi limes,
halved (substitute
with local limes)

This is the holy grail of all sambals in Malaysia. It is the base of so much Chinese and Malay cooking. Often served as a condiment or added to dishes at the start of the cooking process.

Using a mortar and pestle, crush the chillies into a paste. Add the belacan and keep pounding until smooth. (It is okay to have a few chunkier bits in the sambal for texture.)

Just before serving, squeeze over the limes.

Tip: Store in a clean, sterile, airtight container in the refrigerator for up to 2 weeks.

SATAY SAUCE

Spicy peanut sauce

There is nothing worse than making peanut sauce with peanut butter in my opinion. Making satay sauce from scratch is a long process but worth the effort!

MAKES 3 litres (101 fl oz/12 cups)
PREPARATION TIME 30 minutes
COOKING TIME 20 minutes

600 g (1 lb 5 oz/ 3¾ cups) roasted peanuts (see tip)

200 ml (7 fl oz) neutral-flavoured cooking oil

100 g (3½ oz) tamarind purée

600 g (1 lb 5 oz/ 3⅓ cups) grated palm sugar (jaggery)

500 ml (17 fl oz/ 2 cups) coconut milk

100 ml (3½ fl oz) dark cooking caramel (substitute with kecap manis)

SPICE PASTE

30 g (1 oz) candlenuts (substitute with macadamia nuts)

40 g (1½ oz) ground fennel seeds

40 g (1½ oz) ground coriander

50 g (1¾ oz) dried baby shrimp, rehydrated in warm water for at least 15 minutes and drained

50 g (1¾ oz) long red chillies

20 g (¾ oz) dried chillies, seeded, rehydrated in warm water for at least 15 minutes and drained

60 g (2 oz) belacan (shrimp paste), toasted (see tip on page 97)

200 g (7 oz) red Asian shallots, peeled and roughly chopped

100 g (3½ oz) garlic

50 g (1¾ oz) lemongrass stem, white part only, chopped

30 g (1 oz) piece fresh ginger, sliced

30 g (1 oz) piece fresh galangal, sliced

100 ml (3½ fl oz) vegetable oil

Put the peanuts in a food processor and pulse to resemble coarse breadcrumbs.

To make the spice paste, blitz all the spice paste ingredients in a high-speed blender until a smooth paste forms. Set aside.

Heat a wok over a high heat then add the oil. Fry the spice paste until fragrant – this should take 3–5 minutes.

Add 750 ml (25½ fl oz/3 cups) water and let the sauce simmer over a low heat for 10 minutes.

Add the tamarind and palm sugar and mix through. Add the coconut milk and stir to combine. Add the peanuts and caramel and stir to combine. Simmer for a further 5 minutes then remove from the heat.

Tips: If only unroasted peanuts are available, use raw peanuts that have been shelled and skinned, then roast in the oven until golden.

To serve with satay skewers, heat the sauce lightly until warmed.

Store the sauce in clean, sterile, airtight containers in the refrigerator for up to 1 week or freezer for up to 6 months.

Warning: Candlenuts are toxic if consumed raw or undercooked.

SERUNDENG
Coconut floss

Serundeng is a grated coconut condiment often used to accompany rice. You can also mix it through salads and blanched vegetables to add extra flavour.

MAKES 750 g (1 lb 11 oz)
PREPARATION TIME 20 minutes
COOKING TIME 20 minutes

100 ml (3½ fl oz) neutral-flavoured cooking oil, plus extra for the spice paste

250 ml (8½ fl oz/ 1 cup) coconut milk

750 g (1 lb 11 oz) desiccated (shredded) coconut

salt, to taste

SPICE PASTE

50 g (1¾ oz) coriander seeds

50 g (1¾ oz) fennel seeds

50 g (1¾ oz) cumin seeds

200 g (7 oz) tamarind purée

300 g (10½ oz) red Asian shallots

200 g (7 oz) long red chillies

60 g (2 oz) lemongrass stem, white part only, chopped

50 g (1¾ oz) garlic

50 g (1¾ oz) piece fresh ginger, peeled

50 g (1¾ oz) piece fresh galangal, peeled

30 g (1 oz) piece fresh turmeric, peeled

50 g (1¾ oz) candlenuts (substitute with macadamia nuts)

100 g (3½ oz) dried baby shrimp, rehydrated in warm water for at least 15 minutes and drained

Dry-roast all the spices for 5 minutes until fragrant.

To make the spice paste, blend all the spice paste ingredients until smooth. Add in some extra oil or water, if too thick.

Heat a wok over a medium heat then add the oil. Add the spice paste and fry until fragrant, for about 5–7 minutes.

Pour in the coconut milk and simmer to reduce slightly.

Toast the desiccated coconut in a frying pan until golden then add to spice paste mixture. Combine thoroughly. Season with salt.

Tip: Store in a clean, sterile, airtight container in the refrigerator for up to 6 weeks.

Warning: Candlenuts are toxic if consumed raw or undercooked.

03

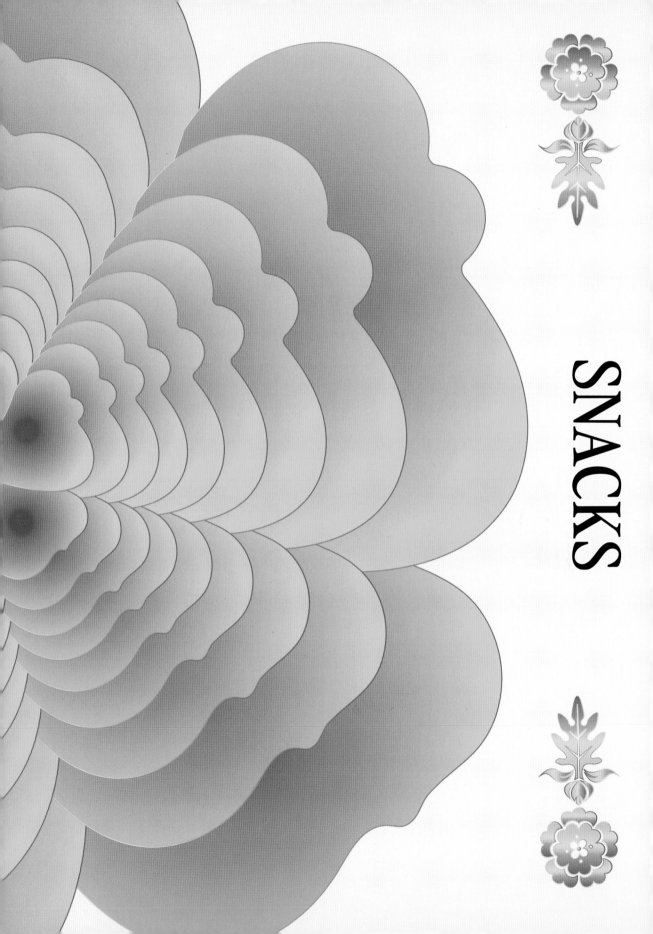

SNACKS

CRISPY FRIED EGG

As basic as it is, I think this is one of the most fundamental recipes in this book to have up your sleeve. So many people don't know how to achieve a crispy fried egg, so here's how.

MAKES 1

COOKING TIME 5 minutes

neutral-flavoured
cooking oil, for
deep-frying

1 × 70 g (2½ oz) egg

light soy sauce,
to taste

ground white pepper,
to taste

Heat the oil in a wok over a medium-high heat. To test if the oil is hot enough, put a wooden chopstick in the oil. If you see tiny bubbles gather around it, the oil is ready. (Alternatively, use a thermometer. It should register between 170–180°C/340–360°F.)

Crack the egg into the centre of the wok. Use a spatula to baste the hot oil over the egg to gently cook the yolk.

Cook for 1–2 minutes until the egg forms a crispy golden edge (or until the yolk is cooked to your liking).

Remove the egg from the wok and season with soy sauce and pepper.

FIVE-SPICED SALT *AND* PEPPER TOFU

The perfect combination of a crispy, fragrant crust and pillowy soft-centred tofu seasoned with a five-spice mix.

SERVES 4
PREPARATION TIME 15 minutes
COOKING TIME 15 minutes

neutral-flavoured cooking oil, for deep-frying, plus 2 tablespoons extra

500 g (1 lb 2 oz) firm tofu, drained

60 g (2 oz) red Asian shallots, finely diced

20 g (¾ oz) garlic, crushed

10 g (¼ oz) long green chillies, finely sliced

5 g (⅛ oz) bird's eye chillies, finely sliced

20 g (¾ oz) spring onions (scallions), finely sliced

salt, freshly ground black pepper and five-spice, to taste

SPICE MIX

70 g (2½ oz) cornflour (cornstarch)

½ teaspoon salt

½ teaspoon ground white pepper

1 teaspoon five-spice

Heat the oil in a wok over a medium-high heat. To test if the oil is hot enough, put a wooden chopstick in the oil. If you see tiny bubbles gather around it, the oil is ready. (Alternatively, use a thermometer. It should register between 170–180°C/340–360°F.)

Meanwhile, cut the tofu into 2 cm (¾ in) cubes. Combine all the spice mix ingredients in a large bowl. Add the tofu and toss to coat.

In batches, gently drop the coated tofu into the hot oil and cook for 3–5 minutes until golden. Remove the tofu with a spider skimmer and drain on paper towel.

Discard the oil and clean the wok. Return the wok to a low–medium heat then add the extra oil. Fry the shallots, garlic and chillies until fragrant.

Return the fried tofu to the wok then add the spring onions. Season with salt, pepper and five-spice.

Serve immediately.

KUIH KERIA
Sweet potato doughnuts

Kuih keria is a Malaysian doughnut made with sweet potatoes and coated in a sweet sugary crust. No baking required and they are completely vegan!

MAKES 12
PREPARATION TIME 20 minutes (+ cooling)
COOKING TIME 10 minutes

200 g (7 oz) orange sweet potato, peeled and cubed

80 g (2¾ oz) plain (all-purpose) flour

neutral-flavoured cooking oil, for deep-frying

200 g (7 oz) caster (superfine) sugar

pinch of salt

Fill a wok with water (enough to boil the sweet potato in). Add the sweet potato, bring to the boil over a high heat and cook for 10–15 minutes until softened. Drain then mash evenly, adding the salt. Set aside to cool to room temperature.

Add the flour and mix well. Shape dough into rings to resemble doughnuts.

Heat the oil in a wok over a medium-high heat. To test if the oil is hot enough, put a wooden chopstick in the oil. If you see tiny bubbles gather around it, the oil is ready. (Alternatively, use a thermometer. It should register between 170–180°C/340–360°F.)

Deep-fry the doughnuts in batches of no more than 4 until they float to the top. Remove from the heat and drain on paper towel. Set aside to cool.

Discard the oil and clean the wok. Add the sugar and 125 ml (4 fl oz/½ cup) water and place over a medium heat. Once the mixture is caramelised – this should take 5–7 minutes – turn off the heat and toss the doughnuts through the syrup to glaze.

Transfer the kuih keria to a serving plate. Allow the doughnuts to cool and the syrup to harden before serving.

JEMPUT JEMPUT
Fried banana dumplings

This is like the Malaysian version of banana cake or bread. Made using ripened bananas, this snack is a popular street food and teatime treat. When your bananas look black and are overripe, they're most likely still good on the inside. Mash them and make these jemput jemput and I guarantee you'll make them again!

MAKES 20
PREPARATION TIME 10 minutes (+ cooling)
COOKING TIME 10 minutes

400 g (14 oz) overripe banana (from about 3 large bananas)

½ teaspoon bicarbonate of soda (baking soda)

pinch of salt

60 g (2 oz) caster (superfine) sugar

150 g (5½ oz/1 cup) plain (all-purpose) flour

neutral-flavoured cooking oil, for deep-frying

icing (confectioner's) sugar, to dust

Peel and mash the bananas thoroughly. (The odd tiny lump is fine.)

Sprinkle the bicarb, salt and the sugar over the banana and mix with a wooden spoon.

Add the flour and stir until combined. (You want a batter that will hug the spoon, then fall off after 2–3 seconds.)

Heat the oil in a wok over a medium-high heat. To test if the oil is hot enough, put a wooden chopstick in the oil. If you see tiny bubbles gather around it, the oil is ready. (Alternatively, use a thermometer. It should register between 170–180°C/340–360°F.)

Drop small balls of batter straight into the hot oil and fry for about 1 minute on each side until golden. (Don't overcrowd the wok.) Remove from the heat and transfer to a plate lined with 2–3 layers of paper towel to drain and cool completely. Repeat with the remaining batter. Dust with icing sugar to serve.

KELEDEK GORENG

Sweet potato fritters

Much like fried banana fritters (pisang goreng) you will find these teatime snacks throughout street stalls in Malaysia. You can make these using different types of sweet potatoes or yams.

MAKES 12
PREPARATION TIME 10 minutes
COOKING TIME 8 minutes

neutral-flavoured cooking oil, for deep-frying

1 × 250 g (9 oz) sweet potato, peeled and cut lengthways into very thin slices (see tip)

Sambal kicap (sweet and salty soy dipping sauce) to serve (see recipe on page 36)

BATTER

150 g (5½ oz/1 cup) plain (all-purpose) flour

1 tablespoon rice flour

1 tablespoon cornflour (cornstarch)

½ teaspoon ground turmeric

¼ teaspoon salt

1 tablespoon caster (superfine) sugar

Heat the oil in a wok over a medium-high heat. To test if the oil is hot enough, put a wooden chopstick in the oil. If you see tiny bubbles gather around it, the oil is ready. (Alternatively, use a thermometer. It should register between 170–180°C/340–360°F.)

Meanwhile, make the batter. Combine all the batter ingredients in a bowl. Gradually pour in up to 270 ml (9 fl oz) water until you get the right batter consistency – thick and not too runny, so that it coats the sweet potato well.

Dip the sweet potato slices in the batter then gently drop them into the hot oil. Fry for 3–4 minutes on each side or until golden. Remove and drain on paper towel.

Serve immediately with sambal kicap.

Tip: If you prefer your sweet potato fritters thicker, be sure to fry for a little longer until the sweet potato has softened.

FRIED HONEY CEMPEDAK

Cempedak is a tropical fruit very similar to jackfruit, but slightly smaller in size. It can be found in many parts of South-East Asia and is often cooked and served as a street-food snack. Cempedak's flavour profile changes when it's cooked.

MAKES 12
PREPARATION TIME 5 minutes
COOKING TIME 10 minutes

neutral-flavoured cooking oil, for deep-frying

12 cempedak

BATTER

350 g (12½ oz/ 2 cups) rice flour

125 g (4½ oz/ 1 cup) cornflour (cornstarch)

75 g (2¾ oz/½ cup) plain (all-purpose) flour

1 teaspoon baking powder

1 × 70 g (2½ oz) egg, beaten

pinch of ground turmeric

pinch of salt

50 g (1¾ oz) butter, softened

500 ml (17 fl oz/ 2 cups) cold soda water (club soda)

Heat the oil in a wok over a medium-high heat. To test if the oil is hot enough, put a wooden chopstick in the oil. If you see tiny bubbles gather around it, the oil is ready. (Alternatively, use a thermometer. It should register between 170–180°C/340–360°F.)

Meanwhile, make the batter. Combine the flours and baking powder in a large bowl. Make a well then add the egg. Add the turmeric and salt and mix through. Add the butter and soda water. Mix to combine.

Add the cempedak to the batter and coat evenly. Gently drop the cempedak into the hot oil and fry until golden. Remove and drain on paper towel.

Serve warm.

SESAME RICE BALLS *WITH* RED BEAN PASTE FILLING

Sesame rice balls, also known as jian dui, are a dim sum favourite. These are filled with red bean paste and coated with toasted sesame seeds.

MAKES 12
PREPARATION TIME 20 minutes
COOKING TIME 5 minutes

60 g (2 oz) white
sesame seeds

90 g (3 oz) soft
brown sugar

250 ml (8½ fl oz/
1 cup) boiling water,
plus extra if required

260 g (9 oz)
glutinous rice flour

150 g (5½ oz)
store-bought sweet
red bean paste

neutral-flavoured
cooking oil, for
deep-frying

Line a baking tray with baking paper then scatter over the sesame seeds. Place a small bowl of water next to the tray.

Dissolve the sugar in the boiling water.

Put the flour in a large bowl. Make a well in the middle and add the sugar mixture. Stir until the dough comes together, adding extra boiling water, if required.

Roll the dough out and divide into 12 pieces. Roll each piece into the size of a golf ball. Make an indentation in the dough ball and fill with 1 teaspoon of red bean paste and shape the dough over the top to seal. Make sure the paste is completely covered. Repeat with the remaining dough balls and red bean paste.

Dip each ball in the bowl of water then roll in the sesame seeds. (This helps the seeds to stick to the dough.)

Heat the oil in a wok over a medium-high heat. To test if the oil is hot enough, put a wooden chopstick in the oil. If you see tiny bubbles gather around it, the oil is ready. (Alternatively, use a thermometer. It should register between 170–180°C/340–360°F.)

Deep-fry the rice balls in batches (make sure to not overcrowd the wok), turning gently with chopsticks or a pair of tongs, for about 2 minutes until the sesame seeds are golden and the balls are cooked evenly. Remove from the oil and drain on paper towel.

Serve warm.

VEGETARIAN SPRING ROLLS

Spring rolls are a classic appetiser at Chinese restaurants. These are made with lots of different Asian mushrooms and water chestnuts, which I love as they give the dish a unique texture and delightful crunch.

MAKES 24
PREPARATION TIME 30 minutes
COOKING TIME 15 minutes

60 ml (2 fl oz/¼ cup) neutral-flavoured cooking oil, plus extra for deep-frying

30 g (1 oz) red Asian shallots, thinly sliced

2 garlic cloves, crushed

150 g (5½ oz) mixed Asian mushrooms (such as shiitake, enoki and wood ear), chopped

100 g (3½ oz) canned water chestnuts, finely diced

1 tablespoon sesame oil

2 tablespoons light soy sauce

30 g (1 oz) Chinese garlic chives, chopped into 5 cm (2 in) lengths

48 spring-roll wrappers

salt and ground white pepper, to taste

sweet chilli sauce to serve

toasted black and white sesame seeds to garnish

Heat a wok over a medium–low heat then add the oil. Fry the shallots and garlic. Add the mushrooms and cook until softened. Season with salt and pepper. Add the water chestnuts and stir to combine.

Pour in the sesame oil and soy sauce. Add the chives and cook until wilted. Remove the wok from the heat and transfer to a bowl to cool. (This is important as the hot mixture will have too much liquid and may tear the wrappers while wrapping.) Discard the oil and clean the wok.

Place the spring-roll wrappers with the pointy ends towards and away from you. Put 1 heaped tablespoon of the filling in the lower half and roll away from you while folding in the sides. Seal with some water at the end. Wrap the spring roll with another wrapper. Repeat with the remaining wrappers and filling.

Heat the extra oil in the clean wok over medium-high heat. To test if the oil is hot enough, put a wooden chopstick in the oil. If you see tiny bubbles gather around it, the oil is ready. (Alternatively, use a thermometer. It should register between 170–180°C/340–360°F.)

Deep-fry the spring rolls in batches for 5–7 minutes until golden. Remove and drain on paper towel.

To serve, dip the warm spring rolls in sweet chilli sauce followed by some sesame seeds.

THAI MUSHROOM LARB *WITH* LETTUCE WRAPS

I came up with this recipe when I decided to do a vegan version of larb and I must say I do love it. It reminds me of a Nyonya dish my mother used to make called jiu hu char, which is jicama, carrots, pork belly, mushrooms and fried cuttlefish served in a lettuce wrap.

MAKES 12
PREPARATION TIME 20 minutes
COOKING TIME 15 minutes

60 ml (2 fl oz/¼ cup) vegetable oil

30 g (1 oz) red Asian shallots, thinly sliced

10 g (¼ oz) garlic, crushed

200 g (7 oz) mixed Asian mushrooms (such as enoki, wood ear, Baby King Brown and oyster), sliced

1 teaspoon caster (superfine) sugar

½ teaspoon chilli powder

1 tablespoon light soy sauce

2 teaspoons fish sauce (coconut amino fish sauce for vegetarian option)

1 tablespoon lime juice

TO SERVE

10 g (¼ oz/⅓ cup) coriander (cilantro) leaves

10 g (¼ oz/½ cup) Vietnamese mint

60 g (2 oz) Lebanese (short) cucumber, julienned

60 g (2 oz) carrot, julienned

12 whole baby cos (romaine) lettuce or mustard greens leaves

Heat a wok over a high heat then add the oil. Fry the shallots and garlic for 1 minute.

Add the mushrooms and cook until they start to break down – this should take 2–3 minutes.

Add the sugar, chilli powder, soy sauce, fish sauce and lime juice. Remove from the heat and transfer the larb to a serving dish.

To serve, place the herbs and vegetables on a large serving plate. Use the lettuce cups as a vessel to eat the larb.

YU CHAR KWAY

Chinese doughnuts

This is the epitome of Malaysian street food. Almost every day you see street vendors selling this crispy, fried, oily bread. It is often served during breakfast and dipped in black coffee.

MAKES 10
PREPARATION TIME 20 minutes
(+ 4 hours resting)
COOKING TIME 10 minutes

400 g (14 oz/
2 ⅔ cups) plain
(all-purpose) flour,
plus extra for dusting

2 teaspoons baking
powder

¼ teaspoon
bicarbonate of soda
(baking soda)

½ teaspoon salt

2 × 70 g (2½ oz)
eggs, lightly beaten
and combined with
water to weigh
250 g (9 oz)

2 tablespoons
neutral-flavoured
cooking oil, plus
extra for coating
and deep-frying

Put the flour, baking powder, bicarb, salt, egg mixture and oil in a freestanding electric mixer. Using the dough hook attachment on a low speed, combine and knead for about 8 minutes until a dough forms.

Rub a little extra oil on your hands (to prevent sticking) to easily remove the dough from the mixer. Divide the dough into 2 equal portions. Shape each portion into a round and smooth ball. Coat with a little extra oil then cover with plastic wrap. Rest the dough at room temperature for no more than 4 hours. (Alternatively, store it in the fridge overnight. The next morning, allow at least 1 hour to bring back to room temperature before using.)

Heat the extra oil for deep-frying in a wok over a medium-high heat. To test if the oil is hot enough, put a wooden chopstick in the oil. If you see tiny bubbles gather around it, the oil is ready. (Alternatively, use a thermometer. It should register between 170–180°C/340–360°F.)

Meanwhile, dust your board or work surface with extra flour. Place 1 dough portion on the board and use your hands to flatten it into a rectangle about 30 cm (12 in) × 15 cm (6 in). Repeat with the remaining dough.

Lightly dust the dough with extra flour (to prevent sticking). Cut each rectangle into 10 equal strips. Lay 1 strip on top of another. Press a chopstick lengthways down the centre to stick them together. Repeat with the remaining dough strips to make 10 in total, dusting with extra flour where necessary.

Once the oil reaches temperature, turn down the heat to low. Gently stretch out the doughnuts to 20 cm (8 in) lengths just before carefully lowering into the oil. (You may cook up to 2 at a time, but do not fry more at once as this will decrease the oil temperature too much.) When they float to the surface, roll them continuously with a pair of chopsticks. Once the doughnuts stop expanding and are golden all over, drain on paper towel. Repeat with the remaining dough strips.

Serve warm or at room temperature.

Tip: To reheat the doughnuts, place in a 200°C (390°F) oven for 10 minutes.

SNACKS

CUCUR UDANG
Malaysian prawn fritters

Cucur udang is a Malay snack served by street vendors during teatime. I think it makes a great canapé or snack when you're having guests over as it holds its crunch really well. The trick is to prepare a thin batter; this way, you'll get all the crispy edges.

MAKES 12
PREPARATION TIME 20 minutes
COOKING TIME 20 minutes

150 g (5½ oz) rice flour

50 g (1¾ oz/ ⅓ cup) plain (all-purpose) flour

2 teaspoons baking powder

1 teaspoon chicken stock (bouillon) powder

pinch each of salt, sugar and ground white pepper

60 ml (2 fl oz/¼ cup) neutral-flavoured cooking oil, plus extra for deep-frying

1 × 70 g (2½ oz) egg

30 g (1 oz) spring onions (scallions), finely chopped, plus extra, thinly sliced, to garnish

250 g (9 oz) raw small prawns (shrimp)

any chilli sauce to serve

Mix all the varieties of flour, baking powder, stock powder, salt, sugar and pepper in a bowl. Add the oil to the mixture and stir to combine.

In a separate bowl, whisk together the egg and 200 ml (7 fl oz) water, then add to the flour mixture. Whisk thoroughly to combine until the mixture is smooth with no lumps. Stir through the spring onions.

Heat the oil in a wok over a medium-high heat. To test if the oil is hot enough, put a wooden chopstick in the oil. If you see tiny bubbles gather around it, the oil is ready. (Alternatively, use a thermometer. It should register between 170–180°C/340–360°F.)

Gently lay a stainless steel ladle in the hot oil and heat for 3 minutes.

Scoop some batter into the ladle then arrange a few prawns on top – as many as you like.

Gently return the ladle to the hot oil and cook until the fritter slides off the ladle. Use a pair of chopsticks to gently turn it over to cook on the other side for a further 3 minutes until the batter is crispy. Remove and drain on a paper towel. Repeat with the remaining batter and prawns.

Sprinkle with extra spring onions and serve with chilli sauce.

FRIED WONTONS

Char wantan or fried wontons are simply moreish. Serve them with any sauce you like. I like mine served with a chilli and garlic dip or some chilli mayo.

MAKES 60
PREPARATION TIME 1 hour
COOKING TIME 15 minutes

60 wonton wrappers

neutral-flavoured cooking oil, for deep-frying

sriracha mayonnaise to serve

FILLING

225 g (8 oz) minced (ground) pork

225 g (8 oz) raw prawns (shrimp), peeled and chopped

20 g (¾ oz) piece fresh ginger, finely grated

30 g (1 oz) spring onions (scallions), finely chopped

2 tablespoons shaoxing rice wine

1 tablespoon light soy sauce

1 tablespoon sesame oil

pinch each of salt and freshly ground black pepper

DIPPING SAUCE

2 tablespoons light soy sauce

1 tablespoon caster (superfine) sugar

10 g (¼ oz) bird's eye chillies, finely sliced

10 g (¼ oz) garlic, crushed

1 tablespoon lime juice

To make the filling, combine all the filling ingredients in a large bowl.

Fill a small bowl with water. Place a wonton wrapper in one hand. Spoon a teaspoon of the filling in the centre of the wrapper. Fold the wrapper over the filling to enclose. Using your fingertip, apply a thin layer of water along the sides of the wrapper and press to seal. Repeat with the remaining wrappers and filling.

If not using the same day, place them on a lined baking tray and freeze overnight. The next day, transfer to containers or zip-lock bags and store in the freezer for up to 6 months, ready to cook from frozen.

To make the dipping sauce, combine all the sauce ingredients in a small bowl and mix until the sugar has dissolved. Transfer to a serving ramekin.

Heat the cooking oil in a wok over a medium-high heat. To test if the oil is hot enough, put a wooden chopstick in the oil. If you see tiny bubbles gather around it, the oil is ready. (Alternatively, use a thermometer. It should register between 170–180°C/340–360°F.)

Deep-fry the wontons in batches of 10, flipping once or twice every minute, until both sides are golden and crispy. Remove and drain on paper towel.

Serve warm with the dipping sauce and sriracha mayonnaise.

IKAN BILIS *AND* BEER NUTS

Anchovies and beer nuts

This is the Malaysian version of salt and vinegar chips or pretzels. This salty and sweet snack goes well with a cold glass of beer. Often, you'll find a version of this served at bars in Malaysia. I think it's a great snack to have handy, and you can most certainly serve it up with other pre-dinner aperitifs.

MAKES 350 g (12½ oz/2 cups)
PREPARATION TIME 10 minutes (+ cooling)
COOKING TIME 20 minutes

180 g (6½ oz) dried anchovies (ikan bilis)

neutral-flavoured cooking oil, for deep-frying, plus 2 tablespoons extra

140 g (5 oz) raw peanuts, skin on

10 g (¼ oz) curry leaves, stems removed, reserve a few leaves for garnish

40 g (1½ oz) white sugar

salt, to taste

SPICE PASTE

50 g (1¾ oz) red Asian shallots, roughly chopped

20 g (¾ oz) long red chillies, seeded and roughly chopped

Preheat the oven to 100°C (210°F).

Rinse the anchovies under cold running water, drain and spread over a lined baking tray. Roast until dry and crisp, for 8–10 minutes.

Heat the oil in a wok over a medium-high heat. To test if the oil is hot enough, put a wooden chopstick in the oil. If you see tiny bubbles gather around it, the oil is ready. (Alternatively, use a thermometer. It should register between 170–180°C/340–360°F.)

Deep-fry the anchovies in batches, stirring frequently, until crisp and golden, for 3–4 minutes. Drain on a paper towel.

Cook the peanuts in the oil until golden and crisp, for 4–5 minutes. Add the curry leaves and cook for 30 seconds. Drain the peanuts and the curry leaves on a paper towel. Discard the oil and clean the wok.

To make the spice paste, blitz the shallots and chillies in a high-speed blender until a smooth paste forms.

Return the wok to a medium heat and add the extra oil. Fry the spice paste, stirring frequently, for 5 minutes. Add the fried anchovies, peanuts and sugar. Season with salt. Cook for another minute until all the moisture from the paste evaporates. Remove from the heat and set aside to cool to room temperature. Add the curry leaves before serving.

04

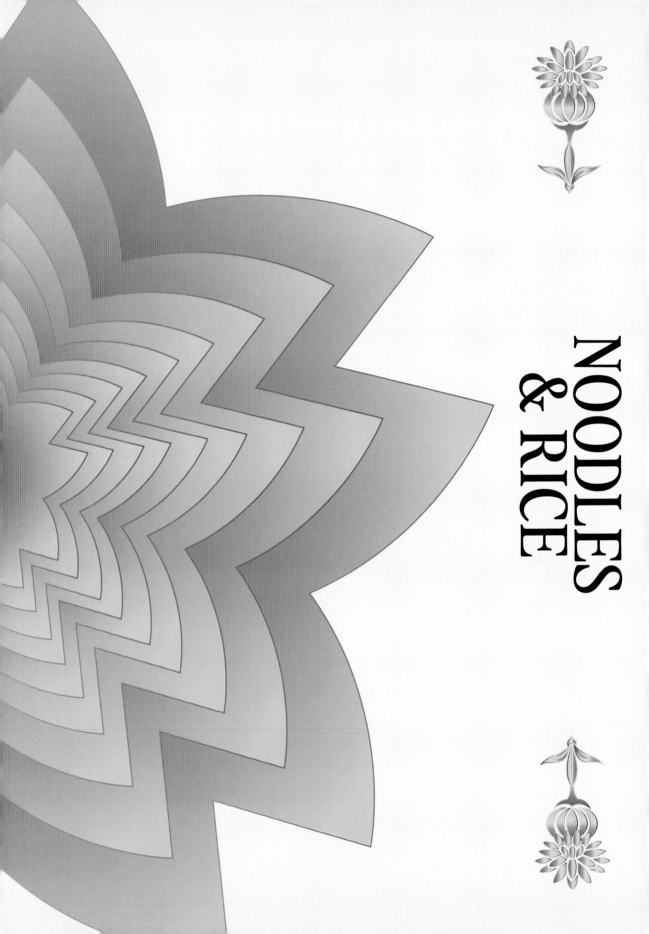

NOODLES & RICE

CHYE TOW KUEH

Carrot cake

This is not the carrot cake we're used to in Western culture. It is actually not made with carrots at all, but rather white radishes, otherwise known as daikon. The name 'chye tow' derives from the Hokkien dialect, meaning white radish. 'Kueh' is the cake and this represents the steamed rice cake rather than the cake that is normally baked.

SERVES 4

PREPARATION TIME 15 minutes
(+ overnight chilling)

COOKING TIME 15 minutes

3 × 70 g (2½ oz) eggs

2 tablespoons neutral-flavoured cooking oil

15 g (½ oz) garlic, crushed

10 g (¼ oz) spring onions (scallions), finely chopped, plus extra, finely chopped, to garnish

1 teaspoon salted pickled turnip (chai poh), soaked in water for a few minutes and drained

1 tablespoon dried chilli paste (chilli boh)

2 tablespoons fish sauce

2 tablespoons light soy sauce

salt and ground white pepper, to taste

any chilli sauce to serve

STEAMED CARROT CAKE

180 g (6½ oz/1 cup) rice flour

40 g (1½ oz) tapioca flour

600 ml (20½ fl oz) chicken stock

300 g (10½ oz) daikon (white radish), grated

1 tablespoon neutral-flavoured cooking oil

5 g (⅛ oz) garlic, crushed

Start by making the carrot cake. Grease a square cake tin. Mix the flours and chicken stock in a large bowl until there are no lumps.

Cook the daikon in a wok of boiling water for 3 minutes until translucent. Drain.

Put the clean wok over a medium heat then add the oil for the carrot cake. Fry the garlic for 30 seconds then add the flour mixture and stir. Add the daikon and mix thoroughly.

Turn the heat to low and continue to stir until the mixture thickens. Remove from the heat and pour the mixture into the prepared tin. Clean the wok.

Fill the wok with 5 cm (2 in) of water and put a metal trivet in the middle of the wok. (The cake tin should be able to float on the surface of the water.) Bring the water to a gentle simmer over a low–medium heat.

Place the tin on top of the simmering water, cover the wok with a domed lid and steam the cake for 1 hour until the top has just set. Top up the water in the wok if needed.

Remove the carrot cake from the heat and set aside in the tin to cool. Refrigerate overnight.

The next day, cut the carrot cake into 3 cm (1¼ in) cubes.

Beat the eggs in a bowl and season with salt and white pepper.

Heat the oil in the wok over a high heat until at smoking point. Fry the cubed carrot cake, turning, until the edges are slightly brown. Push the cake cubes to one side of the wok and add the garlic and spring onions to the other side. Add the pickled turnip, chilli paste, fish sauce and soy sauce. Stir to combine.

Add the beaten eggs and cook until almost cooked through. Toss for 30 seconds to incorporate the egg. Remove from the heat. Transfer to a serving plate and garnish with extra spring onions. Serve with chilli sauce.

CHEE CHEONG FUN
Steamed rice noodle roll

Chee cheong fun is a popular dish served in Cantonese dim sum places. There are a few ways these noodles can be served: with pork or prawns, with fish cakes and fish balls or like this recipe, with a sweet and salty sauce.

SERVES 4

PREPARATION TIME 10 minutes
(+ 45 minutes resting)

COOKING TIME 10 minutes

250 g (9 oz) rice flour

2 tablespoons tapioca flour

1 tablespoon plain (all-purpose) flour

½ teaspoon salt

2 tablespoons neutral-flavoured cooking oil, plus extra to grease

375 ml (12½ fl oz/ 1½ cups) lukewarm water

250 ml (8½ fl oz/ 1 cup) boiling water

toasted white sesame seeds to garnish

Fried shallots (optional) to garnish (see recipe on page 29)

SAUCE

50 ml (1¾ fl oz) hoisin sauce

1 tablespoon sriracha chilli sauce

1 tablespoon Shallot oil (see recipe on page 29)

2 teaspoons roasted sesame paste

Combine the flours and salt in a bowl. Add the cooking oil and lukewarm water and whisk until smooth. Whisk in the boiling water. Set aside for 45 minutes to rest.

Prepare the cake tin. (I use a 25 cm (10 in) square cake tin for steaming the rice noodles.) Very generously brush the bottom and sides of the tin with extra oil.

Fill the wok with 5 cm (2 in) of water and put a metal trivet in the middle of the wok. (The cake tin should be able to float on the surface of the water.) Bring the water to rolling boil then reduce heat to a gentle simmer.

Place the oiled tin on the simmering water to warm it up. Give the batter a good stir then carefully pick up the hot tin and pour in some batter. The noodles should be about 2 mm (⅛ in) thick, so the batter should just cover the bottom of the tin. Swirl it around quickly so it evenly coats the bottom of the tin.

Once the tin is coated, place it on top of the simmering water, cover the wok with a domed lid and steam for 3 minutes until set. Remove the tin from the heat. Working quickly using a pastry scraper, gently roll the rice noodle away from you to create a roll. Cut into 3 cm (1¼ in) lengths or to your desired length. Repeat with remaining batter, greasing the tin between batches and giving the batter a good stir each time before pouring into the tin.

To make the sauce, mix the sauce ingredients in a bowl.

Transfer the rice noodles to a serving dish. Pour over the sauce and sprinkle over some sesame seeds and fried shallots (if using) just before serving.

KOREAN JAPCHAE

Japchae, popular in Korean cuisine, is a savoury and slightly sweet dish made with fried sweet potato glass noodles and vegetables.

SERVES 2
PREPARATION TIME 10 minutes
COOKING TIME 15 minutes

200 g (7 oz) dried sweet potato noodles (dangmyeon)

40 ml (1¼ fl oz) neutral-flavoured cooking oil

30 g (1 oz) red Asian shallots, finely diced

20 g (¾ oz) garlic, crushed

60 g (2 oz) red, yellow or green capsicum (bell pepper), seeded and thinly sliced

50 g (1¾ oz) shiitake mushrooms, thinly sliced (if using dried, rehydrate first)

60 g (2 oz) carrot, julienned

2 tablespoons sesame oil

2 tablespoons light soy sauce

20 g (¾ oz/⅓ cup, firmly packed) baby spinach leaves

salt and ground white pepper, to taste

1 teaspoon toasted white sesame seeds

10 g (¼ oz) red chillies, seeded and sliced

thinly sliced spring onions (scallions) to garnish

Cook the noodles in a saucepan of boiling water for 3–5 minutes until translucent. Drain.

Heat a wok over a high heat then add the cooking oil. Fry the shallots and garlic until fragrant. Add the capsicum, mushrooms and carrot and cook for a further 3 minutes.

Add the sesame oil, soy sauce and noodles and toss through. Stir through the spinach until just wilted. Season with salt and pepper.

To serve, divide the japchae between two bowls. Garnish with the sesame seeds, chillies and spring onions.

MEE SIAM
Siam noodles

In Malaysia you will find two versions of mee siam. One is dry, which is usually served for breakfast, and the other is a more elaborate, wet variation – served with a gravy, usually for special occasions. This recipe shows you both versions.

SERVES 8

PREPARATION TIME 30 minutes (+ 30 minutes soaking)

COOKING TIME 1 hour

300 g (10½ oz) dried rice vermicelli

125 ml (4 fl oz/ ½ cup) neutral-flavoured cooking oil

200 g (7 oz) fermented soybean paste (taucu)

200 g (7 oz/2¼ cups) bean sprouts

100 g (3½ oz) Chinese garlic chives, chopped

NOODLE SPICE PASTE

50 g (1¾ oz) dried red chillies, seeded, rehydrated in warm water for 15 minutes and drained

60 g (2 oz) red Asian shallots, chopped

30 g (1 oz) garlic

60 g (2 oz) dried baby shrimp, rehydrated in water for at least 15 minutes and drained

100 g (3½ oz) raw prawns (shrimp)

GRAVY SPICE PASTE

100 g (3½ oz) red Asian shallots, chopped

50 g (1¾ oz) garlic

30 g (1 oz) dried red chillies, seeded, rehydrated in warm water for at least 15 minutes and drained

65 g (2¼ oz) dried baby shrimp

GRAVY

125 ml (4 fl oz/ ½ cup) neutral-flavoured cooking oil

200 g (7 oz) fermented soybean paste (taucu)

100 g (3½ oz) sugar

2 teaspoons salt

20 g (¾ oz) tamarind slices (asam keping)

120 g (4½ oz/ ¾ cup) peanuts, skins removed, toasted and finely ground

TO SERVE

firm tofu, fried and diced

Chinese garlic chives, chopped into 1 cm (½ in) lengths

boiled eggs, halved

calamansi limes (substitute with local limes), halved

To prepare the vermicelli, soak them in cold water for about 30 minutes until softened. Drain.

To make the noodle spice paste, peel and devein the prawns and chop them into pieces. Blend with the rest of the ingredients in a high-speed blender until smooth.

Heat a wok over a high heat then add the oil. Fry the spice paste, stirring constantly, for 5 minutes until fragrant.

Add the soybean paste and mix well. Put the vermicelli in the wok and use two spatulas to dig in from the sides and lift the mixture up into the middle, coating the noodles with the spice paste along the way. (Try not to break the noodles apart when doing this.) Add the bean sprouts and chives and mix through.

At this stage, should you wish to have the dry version of mee siam, transfer the noodles to a serving bowl and garnish. If you wish to have the wet version served with gravy, please continue with the recipe.

To make the gravy spice paste, blend all the gravy spice paste ingredients and 1.5 litres (51 fl oz/6 cups) water in a high-speed blender until smooth.

To make the gravy, heat a wok over a high heat then add the oil. Fry the gravy spice paste until fragrant and the oil separates – this should take 3–5 minutes. Mix well then add in 100 ml (3½ fl oz) water, soybean paste, sugar, salt and tamarind slices. Just before it comes to the boil, add the ground peanuts. Bring it to the boil over a low heat for about 10 minutes. Remove from the heat.

To serve, transfer the noodles to a serving bowl, spoon over the piping hot gravy and garnish with tofu, chives, egg halves and lime halves.

NOODLES & RICE

SINGAPORE HOKKIEN MEE

Singapore hokkien mee is somewhere in between a noodle soup and a dry noodle dish. It is cooked using a combination of thick rice vermicelli and thin egg hokkien noodles along with vegetables and a slightly viscous prawn and pork stock gravy. It is a favourite of mine at the hawker centres in Singapore.

SERVES 4

PREPARATION TIME 30 minutes
(+ 15 minutes cooling)

COOKING TIME 15 minutes

3 tablespoons neutral-flavoured cooking oil

2 × 70 g (2½ oz) eggs, lightly beaten

250 g (9 oz) fresh hokkien (egg) noodles

150 g (5½ oz) thick rice vermicelli, rehydrated and drained

60 g (2 oz/⅔ cup) bean sprouts

20 g (¾ oz) garlic, crushed

30 g (1 oz) pork fat (optional), cubed and fried until crispy (see KL hokkien mee recipe on page 111)

30 g (1 oz) Chinese garlic chives, cut into 5 cm (2 in) lengths

2 limes, halved

Sambal belacan to serve (see recipe on page 36)

PRAWN STOCK

500 g (1 lb 2 oz) pork bones

200 g (7 oz) raw prawns (shrimp), unpeeled

100 g (3½ oz) squid tubes

1 tablespoon fish sauce, or to taste

1 tablespoon light soy sauce, or to taste

Start by making the prawn stock. Bring 1.5 litres (51 fl oz/6 cups) water to the boil in a large saucepan. Add the pork bones then once it returns to the boil, reduce heat to a simmer. Add the prawns and squid. Cook for 2 minutes then remove the seafood from the pan and set aside to cool.

Once cool enough to handle, peel and devein the prawns, leaving the tails intact. Return the prawn heads and shells back to the pan. Slice the squid to thin rings and set aside.

Meanwhile, continue simmering the broth for 40 minutes.

Strain the broth, discarding the shells and bones. Season the stock with the fish sauce and soy sauce.

Heat a wok over a high heat then add 1 tablespoon of the oil. Add the eggs and scramble quickly with a spatula until almost cooked.

Add the hokkien noodles, rice vermicelli, bean sprouts, 1 tablespoon of the remaining oil and 2 ladles of the prawn stock. Stir-fry over high heat for 1 minute.

Push the mixture to one side of the wok and add another tablespoon of the oil to the other side of the wok. Stir-fry the garlic and lard pieces, if using, for 15 seconds.

Add the chives and mix everything together. Add another 2 ladles of the stock and cover the wok with a domed lid to simmer for 3 minutes.

Remove from the heat. Ladle over the remaining stock and add the prawns and squid. Mix in evenly with the noodles.

Serve with the limes and some sambal belacan on the side.

VEGETARIAN OLIVE LEAF FRIED RICE

I often cook this dish for my friends who are on a vegetarian or plant-based diet. You may choose to remove the eggs completely to make it vegan. Preserved olive leaves impart a lot of umami, which acts as a flavour enhancer, providing saltiness to the dish.

SERVES 4

PREPARATION TIME 15 minutes

COOKING TIME 15 minutes

60 ml (2 fl oz/¼ cup) neutral-flavoured cooking oil

20 g (¾ oz) red Asian shallots, finely chopped

10 g (¼ oz) garlic, crushed

700 g (1 lb 9 oz/ 3¾ cups) cooked jasmine rice (see tip)

2 × 70 g (2½ oz) eggs

30 g (1 oz) spring onions (scallions), finely chopped, plus extra for garnish

70 g (2½ oz) preserved olive leaf, plus extra to garnish

1 tablespoon light soy sauce

salt and ground white pepper to taste

thinly sliced chillies to garnish

Heat the wok over a high heat then add two-thirds of the oil. Fry the shallots and garlic. Add the rice and toss to combine.

Push the rice mixture to one side of the wok and add the remaining oil to the other side of the wok. Beat the eggs in a bowl then add to the wok. Let the eggs sit for 30 seconds before folding through the rice mixture.

Add the spring onions, olive leaf and soy sauce. Toss then season with salt and pepper.

To serve, transfer the fried rice to a serving plate and garnish with some chillies, extra spring onions and extra olive leaf.

Tip: Cook 350 g (12½ oz/1¾ cups) jasmine rice to make about 700 g (1 lb 9 oz/3¾ cups) cooked.

YEE FU MEIN
Long life noodles

Yee fu mein, also known as long life noodles, is very nostalgic for me. My mum would often cook up a Chinese New Year feast with dishes such as kiam chye ak, jiu hu char and braised goose. In addition to those dishes, she would whip up a platter of these delicious slippery noodles. As the name suggests, long life noodles signify longevity in life, as well as prosperity and good luck for the year ahead.

SERVES 4
PREPARATION TIME 15 minutes
COOKING TIME 15 minutes

300 g (10½ oz) dried yee fu noodles

2 tablespoons neutral-flavoured cooking oil

5 g (⅛ oz) garlic, crushed

60 g (2 oz) spring onions (scallions), cut into 5 cm (2 in) lengths

30 g (1 oz) Chinese garlic chives, cut into 5 cm (2 in) lengths

200 g (7 oz) canned straw mushrooms, sliced in half (substitute with other Asian mushrooms)

50 g (1¾ oz) fresh shiitake mushrooms, thinly sliced

250 ml (8½ fl oz/ 1 cup) vegetable or chicken stock

2 tablespoons shaoxing rice wine

2 tablespoons light soy sauce

1 tablespoon oyster sauce (optional)

1 teaspoon sesame oil

ground white pepper to taste

chilli oil or chopped fresh red chillies to serve

Blanch the noodles for 2 minutes in a wok of boiling water to rehydrate. Drain.

Return the wok to a high heat then add the cooking oil. Fry the garlic for 30 seconds to flavour the oil. Add the spring onions, chives, mushrooms and fry for 3 minutes. Pour in the stock and allow to reduce slightly.

Add the noodles and stir well until noodles are evenly coated. Add the shaoxing, soy sauce and oyster sauce, if using, and stir to coat evenly. Add the sesame oil and season with white pepper.

Serve with some chilli oil or fresh chillies.

SANG HAR YEE MEE

Freshwater prawn crispy noodles

Sang har yee mee or freshwater prawn noodles, are one of the most expensive noodle dishes in Malaysia. A plate will set you back around 80–110 Malaysian ringgit (AU$25–35), depending on the serving size and the cost of the prawns. In fact, cooking this dish yourself is much cheaper and in Australia where you get amazing produce it makes the most sense. All you need are a few ingredients like fresh large prawns, ginger, spring onions and some vegetables to cook the thick gravy.

SERVES 4
PREPARATION TIME 15 minutes
COOKING TIME 10 minutes

neutral-flavoured cooking oil, for deep-frying

360 g (12½ oz) crispy yee mee noodles

200 g (7 oz) raw large tiger prawns, peeled and deveined, leaving the heads and tails intact

20 g (¾ oz) piece fresh ginger, thinly sliced

20 g (¾ oz) garlic, crushed

50 g (1¾ oz) red Asian shallots, thinly sliced

30 g (1 oz) spring onions (scallions), cut into 5 cm (2 in) batons, green tops finely chopped for garnish

30 g (1 oz) fresh shiitake mushrooms, sliced (substitute with dried shiitake mushrooms)

70 g (2½ oz) choy sum, cut into 5 cm (2 in) lengths (substitute with Chinese broccoli (kai lan))

1 tablespoon light soy sauce

1 tablespoon shaoxing rice wine (substitute with sherry)

ground white pepper, to taste

pickled green chillies to garnish

EGG CHIFFON SAUCE

500 ml (17 fl oz/ 2 cups) chicken, vegetable or prawn stock

2 teaspoons light soy sauce

1 teaspoon cornflour (cornstarch), mixed into a slurry with 1 tablespoon water

1 × 70 g (2½ oz) egg, lightly beaten

Heat the oil in a wok over a medium-high heat. To test if the oil is hot enough, put a wooden chopstick in the oil. If you see tiny bubbles gather around it, the oil is ready. (Alternatively, use a thermometer. It should register between 170–180°C/340–360°F.)

Fry the noodles for 30 seconds each side until crisp. Remove and drain on paper towel. Transfer to a large serving platter. Reserve 2 tablespoons of the oil in the wok and discard the remaining.

Increase the heat to high and fry the prawns for 3 minutes until cooked through. Remove the prawns and set aside.

Add the ginger, garlic, shallots and spring onions to the wok and fry until fragrant. Add the mushrooms, choy sum, soy sauce and shaoxing. Season with white pepper. Transfer the mixture to the platter.

To make the egg chiffon sauce, return the wok to a medium heat and bring the stock to the boil. Add the soy sauce. Add in a little of the cornflour slurry at a time until the sauce thickens slightly and coats the back of a spoon. Add the beaten egg and swirl to create ribbons.

Pour the sauce all over the noodle mixture. Toss until coated.

Garnish with the spring onion tops and some pickled green chillies. Divide among serving bowls and top with prawns.

MEE GORENG
Fried yellow noodles

There are many variations of this dish throughout South-East Asia. Some regions prefer them sweeter, some more savoury and spicy. This is a Malaysian version using fresh thin egg noodles tossed through a rich, dark and slightly spicy sauce.

SERVES 4

PREPARATION TIME 15 minutes

COOKING TIME 15 minutes

60 ml (2 fl oz/¼ cup) neutral-flavoured cooking oil

30 g (1 oz) garlic, crushed

200 g (7 oz) raw prawns, peeled and deveined, leaving the tails intact

20 g (¾ oz) long red chillies, thinly sliced, plus extra, chopped, to garnish

30 g (1 oz) tomato, cut into wedges

60 g (2 oz) bok choy (pak choy), leaves separated from stems, cut into 8 cm (3¼ in) lengths

50 g (1¾ oz) fish cake, very thinly sliced

500 g (1 lb 2 oz) fresh hokkien (egg) noodles

50 g (1¾ oz) bean sprouts

500 ml (17 fl oz/ 2 cups) chicken stock

60 ml (2 fl oz/¼ cup) kecap manis

60 ml (2 fl oz/¼ cup) chilli sauce

1 tablespoon oyster sauce

pinch of ground white pepper

lime cheeks to serve

Heat a wok over a high heat then add the oil. Fry the garlic for 30 seconds to flavour the oil. Add the prawns and cook for 2 minutes then add the chillies, tomato, bok choy stems and fish cake. Cook and toss for a further minute.

Add the noodles and cook for 3 minutes. Add the bok choy leaves and bean sprouts and cook until just softened.

Add the stock and sauces. Season with pepper. Toss until the noodles are thoroughly coated and heated through.

Divide among serving bowls, garnish with extra chillies and serve with lime cheeks.

MEE GORENG MAMAK

This dish was made popular by the Indian Muslim community that migrated to Malaysia and Singapore many centuries ago, bringing with them a strong Indian influence that has mixed with the local Malay and Chinese influences.

SERVES 4
PREPARATION TIME 15 minutes
COOKING TIME 10 minutes

500 g (1 lb 2 oz) fresh hokkien (egg) noodles

60 ml (2 fl oz/¼ cup) neutral-flavoured cooking oil, plus extra for frying the eggs

30 g (1 oz) garlic, crushed

50 g (1¾ oz) red Asian shallots, sliced

20 g (¾ oz) dried chilli paste (chilli boh)

100 g (3½ oz) potatoes, peeled, boiled and cut into 3 cm (1¼ in) cubes

50 g (1¾ oz) fried bean curd, cut into 1 cm (½ in) slices

50 g (1¾ oz) fish cake (optional), cut into 5 mm (¼ in) slices

200 g (7 oz) squid rings

2 × 70 g (2½ oz) eggs

60 g (2 oz/⅔ cup) bean sprouts

60 g (2 oz) cucumber, diagonally sliced

1 lime, cut into wedges

coriander (cilantro) leaves to garnish

SAUCE

2 tablespoons light soy sauce

2 tablespoons kecap manis

3 tablespoons tomato sauce (ketchup)

1 tablespoon sugar

To prepare the noodles, put them in a colander, pour over some boiling water then drain.

To make the sauce, combine all the sauce ingredients in a jug.

Heat a wok over a high heat then add the oil. Fry the garlic and shallots until fragrant. Add the chilli paste and cook for 30 seconds.

Add the potatoes, bean curd, fish cake and squid rings and cook, stirring, for 2 minutes. Add the noodles and fry for a couple of minutes.

Push the noodle mixture to one side of the wok and add some extra oil to the other side. Crack the eggs into the oil and let them sit for 10 seconds before scrambling and mixing through the noodle mixture. Add the bean sprouts and cook for about a minute. Add the sauce and toss to coat thoroughly. Remove from the heat.

To serve, garnish with cucumber, a wedge of lime and coriander.

NASI GORENG KAMPUNG

Village fried rice

Nasi goreng kampung is a Malay-style fried rice. I particularly love this style of fried rice as it has a lot of texture from the crunch of the beans and the fried anchovies.

SERVES 4

PREPARATION TIME 20 minutes

COOKING TIME 10 minutes

250 ml (8½ fl oz/ 1 cup) neutral-flavoured cooking oil

50 g (1¾ oz) dried anchovies (ikan bilis), rehydrated in room temperature water for 20 minutes and drained to remove excess salt

2 tablespoons fish sauce

1 teaspoon caster (superfine) sugar, plus extra to taste

3 × 70 g (2½ oz) eggs

100 g (3½ oz) snake (yard-long) beans, finely chopped

500 g (1 lb 2 oz/ 1⅔ cups) cooked jasmine rice (see tip)

10 g (¼ oz) green bird's eye chillies, sliced, plus extra to garnish

4 fried eggs (optional) to serve

salt and ground white pepper, to taste

light soy sauce to serve

PASTE

30 g (1 oz) garlic

60 g (2 oz) red Asian shallots, roughly chopped

20 g (¾ oz) dried anchovies (ikan bilis), rehydrated in room temperature water for 20 minutes and drained to remove excess salt

1 teaspoon belacan (shrimp paste), toasted (see tip)

Heat a wok over a medium heat then add the oil. Gently add the anchovies and fry until crispy. Using a strainer, remove the anchovies and drain on paper towel. Remove the wok from the heat, leaving the oil in the wok.

To make the paste, put all the paste ingredients in a high-speed blender and blend until smooth.

Reheat the oil in the wok over a low heat and fry off the paste for 5 minutes until fragrant.

Add the fish sauce and sugar and mix to combine. Crack in the eggs and cook until the whites have just set but the yolks are still runny.

Add the beans followed by the rice and chillies. Toss to combine and season with salt, white pepper and extra sugar. (Remember not to oversalt as the anchovies will be slightly salty.)

Return the anchovies to the wok, reserving a few to place on top as garnish.

To serve, divide the fried rice among serving bowls and garnish with some extra green chillies, a fried egg, reserved anchovies and a drizzle of light soy.

Tips: Cook 250 g (9 oz /1¼ cups) jasmine rice to make about 500 g (1 lb 2 oz) cooked.

To toast the belacan (shrimp paste), place in a frying pan over medium heat and cook, turning frequently, for 5 minutes.

PEARL MEAT NOODLES

Pearl meat is a by-product from pearl cultivation. It was once a humble divers' fare, but these days it commands up to AU$200 per kilogram. It can be eaten raw like sashimi or cooked quickly by searing the meat. The flavour is a combination of abalone and scallop with a delicate and sweet flavour. Cook with noodles and it works a treat.

SERVES 4
PREPARATION TIME 20 minutes
COOKING TIME 10 minutes

60 ml (2 fl oz/¼ cup) neutral-flavoured cooking oil

1 tablespoon crushed garlic

20 g (¾ oz) red Asian shallots, finely sliced

30 g (1 oz) carrot, sliced into very thin disks

50 g (1¾ oz) white cabbage, roughly chopped

80 g (2¾ oz) mixed Asian mushrooms, sliced

150 g (5½ oz) frozen pearl meat (thaw for 15 minutes)

450 g (1 lb) fresh thin egg noodles, rehydrated in hot water for 30 seconds and drained

90 g (3 oz/1 cup) bean sprouts

10 g (¼ oz) Chinese garlic chives, sliced into 5 cm (2 in) lengths

finely sliced spring onions (scallions) to garnish

light soy sauce with thinly sliced fresh chillies to serve

GRAVY

500 ml (17 fl oz/ 2 cups) chicken stock

2 tablespoons oyster sauce

2 tablespoons light soy sauce

1 tablespoon cornflour (cornstarch), mixed into a slurry with 1 tablespoon water

Heat a wok over a medium heat then add the oil. Add the garlic and shallots and fry for 30 seconds to flavour the oil, then add the carrots, cabbage and mushrooms. Cook, constantly tossing, for 5 minutes.

Add the thawed pearl meat and cook for 2 minutes each side. Add the noodles, bean sprouts and chives and mix thoroughly. Transfer the noodle mixture to a serving platter.

To make the gravy, return the wok to a medium heat. Pour in the stock, oyster and soy sauces and bring to a gentle simmer before adding the cornflour slurry. Stir for up to a minute or until thickened. Remove from the heat.

Pour the gravy over the noodle mixture and garnish with some spring onions. Serve with soy sauce and thinly sliced fresh chillies

BEEF HOR FUN

Flat fresh rice noodles with beef

Hor fun noodles fried in a smooth, silky, umami sauce with tender pieces of beef added. What's not to love?

SERVES 4

PREPARATION TIME 10 minutes
(+ 15 minutes marinating)

COOKING TIME 10 minutes

200 g (7 oz) thinly sliced beef eye fillet (substitute with other cuts like flank or rump)

100 ml (3½ fl oz) neutral-flavoured cooking oil

10 g (¼ oz) piece fresh ginger, sliced

10 g (¼ oz) garlic, crushed

100 g (3½ oz) choy sum, leaves and stems separated, cut into 5 cm (2 in) lengths

50 g (1¾ oz) brown onion, sliced

20 g (¾ oz) spring onions (scallions), cut into 8 cm (3¼ in) batons, plus extra, thinly sliced

100 g (3½ oz) bean sprouts, rinsed

2 teaspoons dark cooking caramel (black soy sauce)

pinch of salt

coriander (cilantro) leaves (optional) to garnish

BEEF MARINADE

1 teaspoon sesame oil

2 teaspoons light soy sauce

1 tablespoon oyster sauce

pinch of salt and ground white pepper

2 teaspoons cornflour (cornstarch), mixed with 2 tablespoons water into a slurry

HOR FUN NOODLES

500 g (1 lb 2 oz) fresh thick rice noodles for stir-fries

60 ml (2 fl oz/¼ cup) light soy sauce

2 teaspoons dark cooking caramel (black soy sauce)

1 tablespoon black vinegar

To make the marinade, combine all the marinade ingredients in a bowl.

Add the beef strips to the marinade and set aside for 10–15 minutes to marinate.

Heat the wok over a high heat then add the cooking oil. Fry the beef for 2–3 minutes until 80 per cent cooked through. Transfer the beef to a plate. Reserve the oil in a jug.

To make the hor fun noodles, return the wok to a high heat until at smoking point. Add 2 tablespoons of the reserved oil. Add the noodle ingredients and toss until noodles are evenly coated and slightly charred. Transfer the noodles to a plate.

Add 1 tablespoon of the remaining reserved oil to the wok then stir-fry the ginger, garlic, choy sum stalks and brown onion, tossing frequently, for 2–3 minutes. Add the choy sum leaves and mix well.

Add the beef, spring onions and bean sprouts. Season with the caramel and salt and toss to combine. Add the noodles and toss thoroughly.

Divide among serving bowls. Garnish with some extra spring onions and coriander leaves.

CHAR BEE HOON

Fried vermicelli noodles

This was a staple in the Chan household growing up. When Mum had many bits and pieces of ingredients, she would put them all into a noodle dish much like you would with fried rice. I enjoy having it with a few dashes of Worcestershire sauce, which has a slight piquant and umami flavour.

SERVES 4–6
PREPARATION TIME 20 minutes
COOKING TIME 10 minutes

70 g (2½ oz) pork belly or pork shoulder meat, thinly sliced

60 ml (2 fl oz/¼ cup) neutral-flavoured cooking oil

100 g (3½ oz) raw prawns (shrimp), shelled and deveined, leaving the tails intact

20 g (¾ oz) garlic, crushed

2 × 70 g (2½ oz) eggs, beaten

100 g (3½ oz) choy sum (or any Asian greens of your choice), chopped into 5 cm (2 in) lengths

50 g (1¾ oz/½ cup) bean sprouts

250 g (9 oz) dried rice vermicelli, rehydrated in warm water for 10 minutes and drained

20 g (¾ oz) spring onions (scallions), finely chopped

MEAT MARINADE

1 teaspoon cornflour (cornstarch)

2 teaspoons light soy sauce

1 teaspoon sesame oil

1 teaspoon caster (superfine) sugar

SAUCE

1 tablespoon light soy sauce

1 teaspoon dark cooking caramel (black soy sauce)

1 teaspoon sesame oil

1 teaspoon Worcestershire sauce

Start by preparing your marinade. Combine all the marinade ingredients in a bowl.

Add the pork to the marinade and set aside.

To make the sauce, combine all the sauce ingredients in a jug.

Heat a wok over a high heat then add one-third of the cooking oil. Cook the pork for 3–5 minutes until 80 per cent cooked through. Transfer the pork to a plate.

Leave the wok over a high heat. Add half of the remaining oil then cook the prawns until 80 per cent cooked through then set aside with the pork.

Return the wok to a high heat then add the remaining cooking oil. Fry the garlic for 30 seconds then add the eggs and scramble for 15 seconds.

Add the choy sum and bean sprouts. Toss in the rice vermicelli. (Cut with scissors if too long.) Toss through the pork and prawns. Add the sauce and 60 ml (2 fl oz/¼ cup) water and mix to combine.

Garnish with the spring onions to serve.

SAR HOR FUN

Fried flat rice noodles with egg gravy

This is one of my favourite dishes. Silky wok hei flat rice noodles adopt all the smokiness paired with your protein of choice and vegetables, topped with a thick and slightly viscous egg gravy.

SERVES 4
PREPARATION TIME 15 minutes
COOKING TIME 10 minutes

250 g (9 oz) fresh thick rice noodles for stir-fries

60 ml (2 fl oz/¼ cup) neutral-flavoured cooking oil

2 teaspoons dark cooking caramel (black soy sauce)

60 g (2 oz) thinly sliced pork shoulder (substitute with pork belly or pork neck)

200 g (7 oz) raw king prawns (shrimp), peeled and deveined, leaving the tails intact (substitute with sliced fish cake or squid)

20 g (¾ oz) garlic, crushed

70 g (2½ oz) choy sum, cut into 5 cm (2 in) lengths

1 teaspoon cornflour (cornstarch), mixed into a slurry with 1 tablespoon water

1 × 70 g (2½ oz) egg, beaten

pickled green chillies to garnish

GRAVY

350 ml (12 fl oz) chicken stock

1 tablespoon oyster sauce

1 tablespoon light soy sauce

2 teaspoons dark cooking caramel (black soy sauce)

pinch of ground white pepper

To prepare the noodles, pierce a few holes in the packet then microwave for 30 seconds to soften. Transfer to a large bowl and separate the noodles.

Heat a wok over a high heat then add 1 tablespoon of the oil. Fry the noodles and caramel until charred. (You are looking for slightly browned edges and smoke on the wok.) Remove the noodles and set aside on a plate somewhere warm.

Heat 1 tablespoon of the remaining oil in the wok. Fry the pork for 1 minute before adding the prawns. Mix until just cooked through – about 2–3 minutes. Transfer the pork and prawns to the plate.

Heat the remaining oil in the wok and fry the garlic until fragrant. Add the choy sum and toss for 30 seconds. Add the gravy ingredients and bring to a boil. Reduce to a simmer.

Add the cornflour slurry and egg to the wok and swirl to create ribbons. Remove from the heat then return the noodles, pork and prawns to the wok. Stir until combined.

To serve, garnish with some pickled green chillies.

CHAR KUEY TEOW

*Malaysian fried
flat rice noodles*

I'd be lying if I said that char kuey teow isn't my most-loved fried noodle dish. It's made with flat rice noodles and cooked over very high heat with duck egg, garlic, soy, chilli paste, whole prawns, garlic chives, bean sprouts, Chinese sausage and optional blood cockles. For me, adding lard when you cook the noodles is a must, as is topping it off with some crispy pieces of pork lard just before serving – definitely not a dish to have if you're counting calories!

SERVES 1
PREPARATION TIME 15 minutes
COOKING TIME 7 minutes

2 tablespoons pork lard (substitute with any neutral-flavoured cooking oil), plus extra for frying, if needed

250 g (9 oz) fresh flat rice noodles

20 g (¾ oz) garlic, crushed

1 teaspoon dried chilli paste (chilli boh)

30 g (1 oz) Chinese sausage (lap cheong), sliced

50 g (1¾ oz) raw prawns (shrimp), peeled and deveined, leaving the tails intact

1 × duck egg (substitute with chicken egg)

30 g (1 oz/⅓ cup) bean sprouts

20 g (¾ oz) Chinese garlic chives, chopped

cubed pork fat, fried until crispy (see KL hokkien mee recipe on page 111)

CKT SAUCE

1 tablespoon oyster sauce

1 tablespoon dark cooking caramel (substitute with kecap manis)

2 tablespoons light soy sauce

To make the CKT sauce, combine all the sauce ingredients in a jug.

Heat a wok over a high heat until almost at smoking point then add the lard or oil and swirl around to coat the wok. Add the noodles to char slightly.

Add the garlic and chilli paste and mix through. Add the sausage and prawns and cook for about 30 seconds. Push the noodle mixture to one side of the wok and crack in the egg on the other side. Let it sit for 10 seconds before mixing it through the noodle mixture. Add the sauce and mix to coat thoroughly.

Add the bean sprouts and chives and toss through until just cooked – this should take about 30 seconds. Top with crispy pork fat. Remove from the heat and serve warm.

KL HOKKIEN MEE

The name comes from where the dish originates, Kuala Lumpur. There are several different types of hokkien mee throughout Singapore and Malaysia depending on the state. For example, the Penang hokkien mee is a soup-based prawn noodle dish and the Singapore hokkien mee consists of fried noodles with a thick gravy.

SERVES 4
PREPARATION TIME 30 minutes
COOKING TIME 10 minutes

150 g (5½ oz) pork neck, thinly sliced

450 g (1 lb) fresh hokkien (egg) noodles

50 g (1¾ oz) pork fat, cubed

30 g (1 oz) garlic, crushed

100 g (3½ oz) white cabbage, roughly chopped

thinly sliced spring onions (scallions) to garnish

Sambal belacan to serve (see recipe on page 36)

MARINADE

1 tablespoon light soy sauce

2 teaspoons sesame oil

1 teaspoon cornflour (cornstarch)

pinch of salt and ground white pepper

SAUCE

50 ml (1¾ fl oz) dark cooking caramel (substitute with kecap manis)

2 tablespoons oyster sauce

250 ml (8½ fl oz/ 1 cup) chicken stock (or water)

salt and ground white pepper, to taste

To make the marinade, combine all the marinade ingredients in a bowl.

Add the pork neck, mix well and set aside to marinate.

Put the noodles in a big bowl then pour over boiling water to cover. Stir to break up the noodles then rinse under cold running water and drain.

Heat the wok over a low heat then add the pork fat. (Lard will start to render from the fat.) Lower the heat and slowly cook until the pork fat cubes turn crispy and golden. Remove the crispy pork lard from the wok and set aside on a plate.

Heat the rendered pork lard still in the wok over a high heat until at smoking point. Fry the marinated pork and garlic until fragrant. Stir in the cabbage and cook until slightly softened. Add the noodles and stir to combine.

To make the sauce, combine all the sauce ingredients in a jug.

Add the sauce to the noodles and toss to combine. Cook for a further 5 minutes. (If it looks too dry, add a bit more stock or water.)

Serve the KL hokkien mee with the crispy pork fat, spring onions and some sambal belacan on the side.

YANGZHOU FRIED RICE

This is a basic fried rice that is the foundation of all fried rice dishes. It's basically a mash up of whatever leftovers you have in the fridge and it always hits the spot.

SERVES 4
PREPARATION TIME 10 minutes
COOKING TIME 15 minutes

60 ml (2 fl oz/¼ cup) neutral-flavoured cooking oil

2 × 70 g (2½ oz) eggs, beaten

500 g (1 lb 2 oz/ 2⅔ cups) cooked jasmine rice (see tip)

30 g (1 oz) carrot (fresh or frozen), diced

30 g (1 oz) frozen peas

150 g (5½ oz) Chinese barbecued pork (char siu, substitute with bacon or luncheon meat), diced

100 g (3½ oz) raw prawns (shrimp), halved lengthways, peeled and deveined, leaving the tails intact

30 g (1 oz) spring onions (scallions), finely sliced, green tops thinly sliced for garnish

SEASONING

2 tablespoons light soy sauce

1 teaspoon sesame oil

1 teaspoon chicken stock (bouillon) powder

salt and white pepper, to taste

Heat a wok over a high heat then add the oil. Add the eggs, without stirring, until almost cooked. Add the rice and break up using a spatula. Incorporate the rice with the eggs.

Add the carrot, peas, pork and prawns and toss. Add the seasoning and stir through. Add the spring onions and toss for a few seconds until mixed through.

Serve immediately on a serving platter or large bowl, garnished with the spring onion tops.

Tip: Cook 250 g (9 oz/1¼ cups) jasmine rice to make about 500 g (1 lb 2 oz) cooked.

05

MEAT & POULTRY

KUNG PAO CHICKEN

I love the balance of flavours in this dish. It has crunch from the cashews, sweetness from the vegetables and sauce, and tender pieces of chicken. Definitely a classic to add to everyone's repertoire.

SERVES 4

PREPARATION TIME 15 minutes
(+ 30 minutes marinating)

COOKING TIME 15 minutes

300 g (10½ oz) boneless, skinless chicken thighs, cut into bite-sized pieces

3 tablespoons neutral-flavoured cooking oil

10 g (¼ oz) piece fresh ginger, sliced

10 g (¼ oz) garlic, sliced

5 g (⅛ oz) dried red chillies, seeded, rehydrated in hot water for 15 minutes, drained and chopped

20 g (¾ oz) spring onions (scallions), thinly sliced, green tops thinly sliced for garnish

50 g (1¾ oz) toasted cashew nuts

MARINADE

2 teaspoons light soy sauce

1 tablespoon shaoxing rice wine

1 tablespoon cornflour (cornstarch)

pinch of ground white pepper

1 teaspoon neutral-flavoured cooking oil

KUNG PAO SAUCE

2 teaspoons white sugar

1 tablespoon black vinegar

1 tablespoon light soy sauce

1 teaspoon dark cooking caramel (black soy sauce)

1 tablespoon shaoxing rice wine

1 teaspoon cornflour (cornstarch), mixed into a slurry with 1 tablespoon water

To make the marinade, combine all the marinade ingredients in a large bowl.

Add the chicken, mix well and set aside for 30 minutes to marinate.

Meanwhile, make the kung pao sauce. Combine all the sauce ingredients, except the cornflour slurry, in jug.

Heat a wok over a medium-high heat then add 2 tablespoons of the oil. Fry the chicken for 5–7 minutes until it turns white. Transfer the chicken to a plate.

Return the clean wok to a medium heat and heat the remaining oil. Fry the ginger, garlic and chillies for 30 seconds before adding the chicken back in.

Add the kung pao sauce mixture to the wok and stir to combine. Add the spring onions then pour in the cornflour slurry and simmer, stirring, for 30 seconds. Remove from the heat. Add the cashews and give it a quick toss before transferring it to a serving dish.

Garnish with the spring onion tops.

NYONYA CHICKEN CURRY

I am always delighted by the vibrant colour of this dish and the fragrance it imparts. I like serving it with nasi kunyit (turmeric rice) or you can just serve it with steamed jasmine rice.

SERVES 6
PREPARATION TIME 15 minutes
COOKING TIME 40 minutes

125 ml (4 fl oz/ ½ cup) neutral-flavoured cooking oil

1 kg (2 lb 3 oz) boneless, skinless chicken thighs, chopped

20 g (¾ oz) makrut lime leaves, plus extra, thinly shredded, for garnish

300 ml (10 fl oz) coconut milk

salt, to taste

steamed jasmine rice to serve

SPICE PASTE

100 g (3½ oz) red Asian shallots, roughly chopped

30 g (1 oz) garlic

10 g (¼ oz) dried chillies, rehydrated in hot water for 15 minutes and drained

60 g (2 oz) long red chillies, roughly chopped

60 g (2 oz) piece fresh turmeric, roughly chopped

30 g (1 oz) piece fresh galangal, roughly chopped

To make the spice paste, blend all the spice paste ingredients in a high-speed blender until smooth. Add 1 tablespoon water to get it going, if required.

Heat a wok over a medium heat then add the oil. Fry the spice paste until fragrant – this should take about 5 minutes.

Add the chicken, lime leaves and coconut milk. Mix to combine. Season with salt then cover the wok with a domed lid. Simmer, stirring occasionally, over low heat for 30–35 minutes until cooked through.

Garnish with reserved lime leaves. Serve with rice.

MALAYSIAN FRIED CHICKEN

Everyone has their own interpretation of fried chicken, but what makes this my favourite fried chicken is the spice mix that the juicy tender chicken thighs are coated in. The warm spices in the spice mix pair beautifully with the aroma and citrusy notes from the lemongrass. Deliciously crispy chicken with a crunchy coating on the outside and juicy, tender meat on the inside.

SERVES 6

PREPARATION TIME 15 minutes
(+ 1 hour 10 minutes marinating)

COOKING TIME 30 minutes

1 kg (2 lb 3 oz) boneless chicken thighs, skin on, cut into bite-sized pieces

60 ml (2 fl oz/¼ cup) lemon juice

salt to taste

1 × 70 g (2½ oz) egg

50 g (1¾ oz) cornflour (cornstarch)

neutral-flavoured cooking oil, for deep-frying

chilli sauce and mayonnaise to serve

SPICE PASTE

1 teaspoon black peppercorns

1 teaspoon coriander seeds

½ teaspoon cumin seeds

½ teaspoon fennel seeds

30 g (1 oz) lemongrass stem, white part only, chopped

50 g (1¾ oz) garlic

30 g (1 oz) piece fresh ginger

30 g (1 oz) piece fresh galangal, chopped

10 g (¼ oz) piece fresh turmeric, chopped

Put the chicken in a bowl. Add the lemon juice, season with salt and mix well. Set aside for 10 minutes to marinate.

To make the spice paste, dry-roast the peppercorns, coriander seeds, cumin seeds and fennel seeds until toasted. Remove from the heat and use a mortar and pestle to grind into a powder. Transfer the ground spices to a high-speed blender and add the lemongrass, garlic, ginger, galangal and turmeric and blend until a coarse paste forms. Add 1 tablespoon of water to get it going, if required.

Transfer the spice paste to the chicken bowl and use your hands to thoroughly mix until coated. Set aside for 1 hour to marinate.

Crack the egg into the chicken bowl, add the cornflour and mix well.

Heat the oil in a wok over a medium-high heat. To test if the oil is hot enough, put a wooden chopstick in the oil. If you see tiny bubbles gather around it, the oil is ready. (Alternatively, use a thermometer. It should register between 170–180°C/340–360°F.)

In two batches, gently drop the marinated chicken into the oil and fry until golden and crispy on all sides – this will take about 15 minutes per batch. Strain the fried chicken using a slotted spoon and lay it on paper towel to drain.

Serve immediately with chilli sauce and mayonnaise.

GINGER *AND* RICE WINE CHICKEN

Confinement is a period for the body to recuperate from childbirth, and in the past when infant and maternal mortality rates were high, mums and babies were kept indoors to prevent them from getting ill. It usually lasted for thirty days after birth and one of the common Chinese confinement practices was eating foods that were right for the body, such as ginger and rice wine chicken.

This dish contains a copious amount of ginger, which helps with blood circulation and to expel 'wind'; wine, for keeping the body warm; and chicken, for its high protein content.

SERVES 6
PREPARATION TIME 10 minutes
COOKING TIME 1 hour

1 tablespoon sesame oil

100 g (3½ oz) fresh ginger, preferably older ginger, peeled and bruised

1 × 1.5 kg (3 lb 5 oz) chicken, chopped into bite-sized pieces

400 ml (13½ fl oz) Chinese yellow rice wine

200 ml (7 fl oz) Chinese white rice wine

50 g (1¾ oz) caster (superfine) sugar

salt to taste

10 g (¼ oz) dried goji berries, rehydrated in water for 15 minutes and drained

steamed jasmine rice to serve

spring onions (scallions) or coriander (cilantro) leaves to garnish

Heat a wok over a medium heat then add the oil. Fry the ginger for 3–5 minutes until fragrant. Add the chicken and cook, tossing frequently, for a further 5 minutes until the chicken has some colour.

Mix in the rice wines and bring to the boil. Add the sugar and season with salt then bring to a simmer over low heat. Cover the wok with a domed lid and cook for 45 minutes.

Add the goji berries and simmer for a further 5 minutes.

Remove from the heat and serve hot with rice, garnished with some spring onions or coriander.

AYAM MASAK MERAH

Red chicken

A popular Malay casserole dish in Malaysia, chicken pieces are cooked with lots of aromatics, which impart a lot of flavour. It is simmered in passata to give it the vibrant red colour.

SERVES 6

PREPARATION TIME 20 minutes (+ 10 minutes marinating)

COOKING TIME 40 minutes

1 × 1.5 kg (3 lb 5 oz) chicken, chopped into bite-sized pieces

1 teaspoon ground turmeric

salt to taste

neutral-flavoured cooking oil, for frying

5 g (⅛ oz) curry leaves

100 g (3½ oz) tamarind pulp

150 g (5½ oz) tomato passata (puréed tomatoes)

100 g (3½ oz) chilli sauce

40 g (1½ oz) grated palm sugar (jaggery)

2 tablespoons oyster sauce

Fried shallots to garnish (see recipe on page 29)

coriander (cilantro) leaves to garnish

SPICE PASTE

30 g (1 oz) piece fresh ginger, sliced

150 g (5½ oz) red Asian shallots, chopped

50 g (1¾ oz) garlic

60 g (2 oz) lemongrass stem, white part only, chopped

10 g (¼ oz) dried red chillies, seeded, rehydrated in hot water for 15 minutes and drained

60 g (2 oz) long red chillies, seeded and chopped

To make the spice paste, blitz all the spice paste ingredients in a high-speed blender until smooth. Add a couple of tablespoons of water to get it going, if required.

Put the chicken in a large bowl. Add the turmeric and season well with salt. Set aside for 10 minutes to marinate.

Heat a wok over a medium heat then add the oil. In batches, gently lay the chicken in the hot oil and fry for 10 minutes until cooked through. Remove and drain on paper towel.

Leave about 2 tablespoons worth of oil in the wok and discard the rest. Return the wok to a medium heat and fry the spice paste for 3–5 minutes until fragrant.

Add the curry leaves followed by the tamarind, passata, chilli sauce, palm sugar, oyster sauce and 250 ml (8½ fl oz/1 cup) water. Simmer over low heat for 10 minutes.

Add the fried chicken and mix to coat the chicken in sauce. Stir for a further 3 minutes then remove from the heat.

To serve, transfer the chicken to a serving dish and garnish with some fried shallots and coriander.

LOR ARK
Teochew braised duck

Lor ark exemplifies the Teochew cooking method, which emphasises the preservation of the original flavours of the ingredients and employs techniques like braising and slow cooking. This dish is often served during festive times such as Chinese New Year or on special occasions.

SERVES 6
PREPARATION TIME 15 minutes
COOKING TIME 1 hour 50 minutes

1 × 1.5 kg (3 lb 5 oz) duck

1 lemon, sliced in half

3 tablespoons neutral-flavoured cooking oil

100 g (3½ oz) piece fresh galangal, cut into thick slices

100 g (3½ oz) piece fresh ginger, cut into thick slices

70 g (2½ oz) garlic, bruised

2 cinnamon sticks, crushed

1 teaspoon cloves

5 g (⅛ oz) star anise

3 bay leaves

1 teaspoon ground white pepper

1 teaspoon five-spice

50 g (1¾ oz/¼ cup) soft brown sugar

150 ml (5 fl oz) dark cooking caramel (black soy sauce)

salt, to taste

Chilli vinegar sauce to serve (see recipe on page 28)

Start by seasoning the duck. Use the lemon halves to rub in the cavity of the duck and all over the skin. Season liberally with salt. Give the duck a good rinse and pat dry. Now, the duck is ready to be cooked.

Heat a wok over a medium heat then add the oil. Fry the galangal, ginger, garlic, cinnamon, cloves, star anise, bay leaves, white pepper, five-spice, sugar and caramel. Mix through until fragrant.

Add the duck and baste with the sauce mixture. Once the duck has a little bit of colour on the skin, pour in 250 ml (8½ fl oz/1 cup) water. Turn the heat to low, cover the wok with a domed lid and simmer for 15 minutes.

Turn the duck over and if the water level is below 2 cm (¾ in), pour in a bit more water. (You want the duck to simmer gently in the sauce.) Cover and cook for a further 90 minutes, turning the duck every 15 minutes to achieve an even cook. Each time, check the water level and add more, if required.

Once it's cooked, remove the lid and season with salt. Gently lift the duck from the wok and transfer to a large serving plate.

Slice and serve with some chilli vinegar sauce.

MUI CHOY
Pork with mustard greens

Mui choy is preserved mustard greens and there are two types – one is salty while the other is sweet. Here, it is braised with pieces of pork in a rich sweet and savoury sauce.

SERVES 6
PREPARATION TIME 15 minutes
COOKING TIME 2 hours 10 minutes

500 g (1 lb 2 oz) dried salted mustard greens, rehydrated in water for 10 minutes and drained

250 g (9 oz) dried sweet mustard greens, rehydrated in water for 10 minutes and drained

1 garlic bulb

60 ml (2 fl oz/¼ cup) neutral-flavoured cooking oil

500 g (1 lb 2 oz) pork shoulder, cut into 3 cm (1¼ in) cubes

500 g (1 lb 2 oz) pork belly, cut into 6 mm (¼ in) slices

5 g (⅛ oz) ground white pepper

60 ml (2 fl oz/ ¼ cup) dark cooking caramel (black soy sauce)

60 g (2 oz/⅓ cup) soft brown sugar

125 ml (4 fl oz/ ½ cup) light soy sauce

salt and ground white pepper, to taste

plain congee to serve

Slice the mustard greens into 3 cm (1¼ in) lengths.

Peel and finely chop 3 garlic cloves, bruising the rest in its skin.

Heat a wok over a medium heat then add the oil. Fry the bruised whole garlic cloves until fragrant. Add the pork, chopped garlic, pepper and caramel. Turn the heat down to low and simmer for 15 minutes, stirring frequently.

Add the mustard greens and stir to mix through. Cook for 5 minutes before adding the sugar. Add enough water to cover the pork and cook with the lid slightly ajar for 1 hour and 30 minutes, checking the level of the liquid every 15 minutes.

Once the meat has been cooking, taste and season with salt and pepper. Add the soy sauce a little at a time to avoid making it too salty. Stir and allow to simmer for another 15 minutes before removing from the heat.

Serve with congee.

MEAT & POULTRY

TAU YEW BAK
Pork braised in soy

Tau yew bak is a traditional Hokkien dish consisting of slow-cooked pork in warm spices and light and dark soy sauces, and usually served with hard-boiled eggs. There is also a generous amount of garlic – usually a whole bulb is used when cooking this dish.

SERVES 6
PREPARATION TIME 10 minutes
COOKING TIME 50 minutes

60 ml (2 fl oz/¼ cup) neutral-flavoured cooking oil

1 garlic bulb, cloves separated but not peeled, plus 20 g (¾ oz) extra, crushed

10 g (¼ oz) white peppercorns, cracked or smashed

750 g (1 lb 11 oz) pork shoulder or pork belly, cut into 3 cm (1¼ in) pieces

100 ml (3½ fl oz) dark cooking caramel (black soy sauce)

2 teaspoons white sugar

10 g (¼ oz) cinnamon stick

5 g (⅛ oz) star anise

1 teaspoon cloves

salt to taste

4 hard-boiled eggs, peeled and halved

steamed jasmine rice to serve

thinly sliced spring onions (scallions) to garnish

Heat a wok over medium heat then add the oil. Fry the garlic cloves and peppercorns until fragrant.

Add the pork and fry to seal in the juices – this should take about 3 minutes.

Mix through the extra crushed garlic, followed by the caramel, sugar and 250 ml (8½ fl oz/1 cup) water. Add the cinnamon, star anise and cloves. Bring to the boil then reduce heat to low. Cover and simmer for 40–45 minutes until the pork is tender.

Add the eggs and sit in the sauce for a minute, turning occasionally, to absorb the colour of the sauce. Remove from the heat.

Serve warm with rice, garnished with some spring onions.

PAI GUAT WONG

Sticky pork ribs

Sweet and sour pork ribs is a Cantonese classic. Simply put, it's finger licking good!

SERVES 6

PREPARATION TIME 10 minutes
(+ 30 minutes marinating)

COOKING TIME 20 minutes

500 g (1 lb 2 oz)
pork spare ribs

neutral-flavoured
cooking oil, for
deep-frying, plus
1 tablespoon extra

cornflour (cornstarch),
for coating

30 g (1 oz) garlic,
finely chopped

60 g (2 oz) spring
onions (scallions),
finely chopped

MARINADE

1 teaspoon cornflour
(cornstarch)

1 × 70 g (2½ oz) egg

2 teaspoons sesame
oil

20 g (¾ oz)
fermented soybean
paste (taucu)

½ teaspoon ground
white pepper

salt, to taste

SAUCE

40 g (1½ oz) tomato
sauce (ketchup)

20 g (¾ oz) plum
sauce

1 tablespoon light
soy sauce

2 teaspoons
Worcestershire
sauce

20 g (¾ oz) soft
brown sugar

To make the marinade, combine all the marinade ingredients in a large bowl.

Add the pork ribs and set aside for at least 30 minutes to marinate.

Meanwhile, make the sauce. Combine all the sauce ingredients with 2 tablespoons water in a bowl.

Heat the cooking oil in a wok over medium-high heat. To test if the oil is hot enough, put a wooden chopstick in the oil. If you see tiny bubbles gather around it, the oil is ready. (Alternatively, use a thermometer. It should register between 170–180°C/340–360°F.)

Lightly coat the marinated ribs with cornflour and deep-fry in batches until crispy and golden. Drain on paper towel.

In a clean wok, heat the extra cooking oil over medium heat. Fry the garlic for 30 seconds to flavour the oil. Add the sauce and simmer over low heat for 10 minutes.

Add the fried ribs to the wok and simmer for up to a minute, coating the ribs in the sauce. Add the spring onions and mix through.

Transfer the ribs to a serving platter. Top with spring onions to serve.

BEEF MURTABAK

Beef murtabak, a crispy, buttery roti stuffed with beef flavoured with warm spices, is a dish served by the Indian Muslim community in Malaysia and Singapore. You can mix up the protein and use lamb or chicken mince instead.

SERVES 4–6

PREPARATION TIME 15 mins (+ cooling)

COOKING TIME 10 minutes

100 ml (3½ fl oz) neutral-flavoured cooking oil, plus extra for frying

60 g (2 oz) red onion, finely diced

20 g (¾ oz) garlic, crushed

300 g (10½ oz) minced (ground) beef

1 teaspoon ground turmeric

1 teaspoon chilli powder

1 teaspoon ground cumin

1 teaspoon ground fennel

4 × 70 g (2½ oz) eggs, beaten

4 pieces of frozen roti canai dough

100 g (3½ oz) butter

salt and ground white pepper, to taste

Heat the oil in a wok over medium-low heat. Fry the onion and garlic until the onion turn translucent. Add the beef and mix well. Add the spices and stir to combine. Cook for 5 minutes then season with salt and pepper. Remove from the heat and transfer the beef filling to a bowl to cool slightly.

Add the beaten eggs to the beef filling. Stir until well combined.

Thaw the frozen roti canai for 15–30 minutes. Using a rolling pin, slightly flatten the dough pieces until thin. Pour some of the beef mixture over the skin and roll into a log, then shape into a coil and flatten it out again.

Place the wok over low heat and add 15–20 g of butter per piece and extra oil. Fry for 2–3 minutes on each side until golden.

Slice into whatever shape pieces you fancy and serve.

06

SEAFOOD

BLACK PEPPER CRABS

Black pepper crabs are gutsy with a big punch in the face full of flavour. It's a popular dish served in Malaysia and Singapore. It's the lesser known sister of the famous chilli crabs. I source mud crabs from my seafood supplier Tim and Terry Oyster Supply in far North Queensland. I'd always recommend getting them live but if you can't, fresh or frozen are still okay.

SERVES 6

PREPARATION TIME 20 minutes

COOKING TIME 20 minutes

neutral-flavoured cooking oil, for deep-frying

2 kg (4 lb 6 oz) mud crabs, gills removed, cleaned and broken cut into smaller pieces

BLACK PEPPER SAUCE

20 g (¾ oz) black peppercorns, toasted and ground into a coarse powder

50 g (1¾ oz) red Asian shallots, finely sliced

20 g (¾ oz) piece fresh ginger, julienned

20 g (¾ oz) garlic, crushed

10 g (¼ oz) curry leaves

10 g (¼ oz) long red chilli, finely sliced

10 g (¼ oz) dried chillies

2 teaspoons white sugar

2 tablespoons oyster sauce

1 tablespoon soy sauce

1 tablespoon dark cooking caramel (substitute with kecap manis)

Heat the oil in a wok over medium-high heat. To test if the oil is hot enough, put a wooden chopstick in the oil. If you see tiny bubbles gather around it, the oil is ready. (Alternatively, use a thermometer. It should register between 170–180°C/340–360°F.)

To clean the crab, crack the shell with something heavy like a pestle so that it is easier to remove the flesh. Pull the apron off. The 'apron' is the triangle shell on the bottom of the crab. This should also remove the shell from the front. Once the top shell is gone, you'll see the crab's insides. Along the top are two rows of opaque, feathery gills. Pull them off and discard them. The mandibles, at the front of the crab, can be removed simply by snapping them off. Discard these also. Rinse under running water. Break the body in half and remove the claws.

Gently add the crab pieces to the wok one at a time and cook until the shells turn bright red, turning every few minutes – this should take 8–10 minutes, depending on the size of your crabs. Drain on a paper towel.

Discard the excess oil from the wok, leaving about 2 tablespoons of the oil in the wok.

To make the sauce, return the wok to high heat and fry the peppercorns for 30 seconds until fragrant. Add the shallots, ginger, garlic, curry leaves and chillies and fry for 1–2 minutes until fragrant.

Add the sugar, oyster sauce, soy sauce and caramel and stir to combine. Add the crab pieces and toss to coat evenly. Remove from the heat and you're ready to serve.

Note: The most humane way to kill a fresh crab is to place it in the freezer for an hour or two to lower its body temperature so it falls asleep. You can also stab it through the rear nerve centre with a sharp knife.

CHILLI CRABS

There is an ongoing debate about the origins of chilli crabs. Is it a Malaysian or Singaporean dish? Safe to say, Singapore has owned this dish and made it popular on an international level. It doesn't bother me where it originated from. The key to making a good chilli crab is of course the crab but also a more textured, sweet and savoury tomato and chilli based sauce. Of course the pièce de résistance are the mantou buns, which are usually served steamed or fried to mop up all that goodness.

SERVES 6
PREPARATION TIME 30 minutes
COOKING TIME 30 minutes

neutral-flavoured cooking oil, for deep-frying

2 kg (4 lb 6 oz) large mud crabs, gills removed, cleaned and broken cut into smaller pieces (see method on page 141)

1 tablespoon fermented soybean paste (taucu)

170 g (6 oz) tomato passata (puréed tomatoes)

125 ml (4 fl oz/ ½ cup) tomato sauce (ketchup)

2 tablespoons rice vinegar

60 g (2 oz) caster (superfine) sugar

2 teaspoons cornflour (cornstarch), mixed into a slurry with 1 tablespoon water

1 × 70 g (2½ oz) egg

SPICE PASTE

70 g (2½ oz) long red chillies, chopped

100 g (3½ oz) red Asian shallots

30 g (1 oz) garlic

10 g (¼ oz) piece fresh ginger, sliced

10 g (¼ oz) piece fresh galangal, sliced

20 g (¾ oz) lemongrass, white part only, chopped

20 g (¾ oz) belacan (shrimp paste), toasted (see tip on page 99)

30 g (1 oz) dried baby shrimp, rehydrated in hot water for at least 15 minutes and drained

Start by preparing your spice paste. Blend all the spice paste ingredients in a high-speed blender until smooth.

Heat the oil in a wok over medium-high heat. To test if the oil is hot enough, put a wooden chopstick in the oil. If you see tiny bubbles gather around it, the oil is ready. (Alternatively, use a thermometer. It should register between 170–180°C/340–360°F.)

Gently add the crab pieces to the wok one at a time and cook until the shells turn bright red, turning every few minutes – this should take 8–10 minutes, depending on the size of your crabs. Drain on paper towel.

Discard the excess oil from the wok, leaving about 2 tablespoons of oil in the wok. Return the wok to medium heat and fry the spice paste until fragrant, about 5 minutes.

Add the soybean paste, passata, tomato sauce, vinegar, sugar and 500 ml (17 fl oz/2 cups) water. Allow to simmer for 10–15 minutes until the sauce thickens slightly.

Pour in the cornflour slurry. Allow to thicken further over low heat before cracking in the egg and swirling it clockwise in the sauce to create ribbons.

Add the crab pieces back in and toss to coat evenly.

Tips: Prepare the spice paste up to a day ahead and store in a clean, sterile airtight container in the refrigerator.

The sauce will keep in a clean, sterile, airtight container in the refrigerator for up to 1 week.

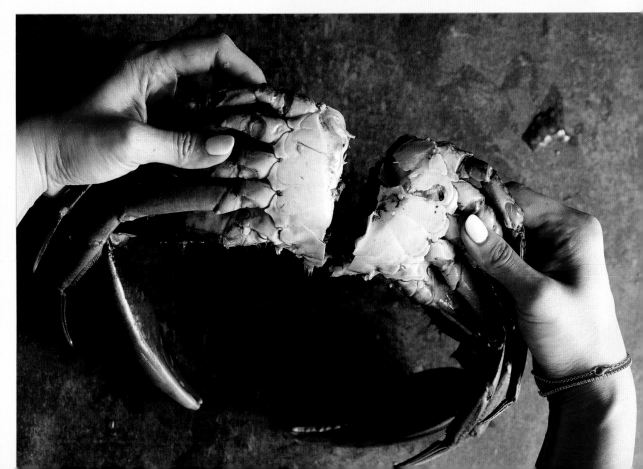

KAM HEONG CRABS

Golden fragrance crabs

When we were kids, I remember tagging along with my dad to the outdoor night market called 'pasar malam' to buy fresh seafood. I watched my dad as he picked out the strongest crabs of the bunch. We would take them home and kill and clean them just before cooking. We would have fresh live crabs cooked in different ways, but kam heong was one of my favourites. Kam heong means golden fragrance, and the fragrance comes from the fried curry leaves and little baby shrimps that impart next-level kind of umami. That paired with some curry powder is like the best fusion of flavours in one dish.

SERVES 6–8
PREPARATION TIME 20 minutes
COOKING TIME 25 minutes

neutral-flavoured cooking oil, for deep-frying

2 kg (4 lb 6 oz) large mud crabs, gills removed, cleaned and broken cut into smaller pieces

50 g (1¾ oz) dried baby shrimp, rehydrated in warm water for 10 minutes and drained

6 dried chillies, rehydrated in hot water for 15 minutes and drained

2–3 bird's eye chillies, chopped

30 g (1 oz) red Asian shallots, finely diced

20 g (¾ oz) garlic, finely diced

15 g (½ oz) curry leaves

1 tablespoon fish curry powder

1 teaspoon cracked black pepper

30 g (1 oz) soft brown sugar

60 ml (2 fl oz/¼ cup) dark cooking caramel (black soy sauce)

2 tablespoons oyster sauce

2 tablespoons soy sauce

coriander (cilantro) leaves and thinly sliced spring onions (scallions) to garnish

Heat the oil in a wok over high heat. To test if the oil is hot enough, put a wooden chopstick in the oil. If you see tiny bubbles gather around it, the oil is ready. (Alternatively, use a thermometer. It should register between 170–180°C/340–360°F.)

Meanwhile, crack the crab shells with something heavy like a pestle so that it is easier to remove the flesh.

Gently add the crab pieces to the wok one at a time and cook until the shells turn bright red, turning every few minutes – this should take 8–10 minutes, depending on the size of your crabs. Drain on paper towel.

Discard the excess oil from the wok, leaving about 2 tablespoons of oil in the wok. Return the wok to high heat and fry the shrimp until crispy then add the chillies, shallots, garlic and curry leaves and fry until fragrant. Add the curry powder, pepper and sugar. Toss to combine.

Add the caramel, oyster sauce, soy sauce and 250 ml (8½ fl oz/1 cup) water. Stir until combined and dripping consistency, adding more water if necessary.

Serve garnished with coriander and spring onion.

WHITE PEPPER CRABS

The natural sweetness of the crabs is enhanced by the robust, peppery flavour of the sauce they swim in.

SERVES 6–8
PREPARATION TIME 30 minutes
COOKING TIME 25 minutes

2 kg (4 lb 6 oz) mud crabs, cleaned, gills removed and broken into smaller pieces

30 g (1 oz) freshly ground white peppercorns

60 g (2 oz) butter, cubed

60 ml (2 fl oz/¼ cup) neutral-flavoured cooking oil

30 g (1 oz) piece fresh ginger, sliced

100 g (3½ oz) small red Asian shallots, finely sliced

60 g (2 oz) garlic, finely chopped

250 ml (8½ fl oz/ 1 cup) shaoxing rice wine

500 ml (17 fl oz/ 2 cups) chicken stock

60 g (2 oz) spring onions (scallions), chopped into 5 cm (2 in) lengths plus extra, thinly sliced, for garnish

1 teaspoon cornflour (cornstarch), mixed into a slurry with 2 tablespoons water

salt and caster (superfine) sugar to taste

Crack the crab shells with something heavy like a pestle so that it is easier to remove the flesh.

Heat a wok over high heat. Toast the peppercorns for a few seconds before adding the butter and oil. Once the butter has melted, add the ginger and shallots and toss through.

Add the garlic and stir through for 30 seconds then pour in the shaoxing and stock. Add the crabs. Cover the wok with a domed lid and cook, stirring halfway through, for 5–7 minutes until cooked through.

Add the spring onions. Check the seasoning. If needed, add in salt and sugar to taste.

Pour in the cornflour slurry and allow to thicken over the heat. Once thickened, remove from the heat.

Transfer to a serving bowl and garnish with extra spring onion.

SOTONG GORENG

Fried squid

Slightly chewy in the middle, coated with a crispy batter. I always say the smaller the squid the better!

SERVES 6
PREPARATION TIME 20 minutes
COOKING TIME 15 minutes

neutral-flavoured cooking oil, for deep-frying

350 g (12½ oz) squid tubes, cut into thick rings

salt, to season

lime or lemon wedges to serve

Chilli vinegar sauce (or any sauce of your liking) to serve (see page 26)

finely chopped coriander (cilantro) leaves to garnish

WET BATTER

1 × 70 g (2½ oz) egg

pinch of salt, caster (superfine) sugar and ground turmeric

DRY BATTER

60 g (2 oz) plain (all-purpose) flour

75 g (2¾ oz) rice flour

salt and caster (superfine) sugar to taste

To clean the squid, remove the head from the body by pulling them apart. You will end up with the head, innards and the body tube. The tentacles and body tube are edible, while the head behind the tentacles and the innards should be discarded. (Note: if you plan on eating the tentacles, you must remove the beak. The beak is a bony piece of inedible cartilage that is located at the base of the tentacles where they connect to the head of the squid. Once the tentacles are cut from the head, squeeze the connective tissue at the top and the beak will easily come out.)

Remove the cartilage from the squid. The cartilage looks like a clear shard of glass and is inedible. Simply pull it from the body tube and discard it. You can eat the brownish-purple spotty skin on the body or you can remove it by making a small incision and pulling it off. Now you have a fully cleaned squid tube that you can cut however you wish.

To make the wet batter, combine all the wet batter ingredients in a bowl.

In a separate bowl, combine all the dry batter ingredients.

Heat the oil in a wok over medium-high heat. To test if the oil is hot enough, put a wooden chopstick in the oil. If you see tiny bubbles gather around it, the oil is ready. (Alternatively, use a thermometer. It should register between 170–180°C/340–360°F.)

Meanwhile, coat the squid in the dry batter and shake off excess. Dip into the wet batter, allowing excess to drip off.

In batches, deep-fry the squid, turning, until golden – this should take 2–3 minutes.

Transfer to a serving dish and squeeze over some lemon or lime just before serving. Season with salt. Serve with Chilli vinegar sauce, garnished with coriander.

SQUID SAMBAL

Serve this with nasi lemak or just plain rice with a squeeze of calamansi lime juice.

SERVES 6
PREPARATION TIME 20 minutes
COOKING TIME 10 minutes

60 ml (2 fl oz/¼ cup) neutral-flavoured cooking oil

600 g (1 lb 5 oz) squid tubes, cut into bite-sized pieces

2 tablespoons lime juice

3 tablespoons tomato sauce (ketchup)

1 tablespoon caster (superfine) sugar

salt, to taste

steamed jasmine rice and calamansi lime halves (substitute with local limes) to serve

SPICE PASTE

30 g (1 oz) long red chillies, seeded and chopped

5 g (⅛ oz) dried chillies, seeded, rehydrated in hot water for 15 minutes and drained

60 g (2 oz) red onion, chopped

10 g (¼ oz) garlic

20 g (¾ oz) belacan (shrimp paste), toasted (see tip on page 99)

5 g (⅛ oz) piece fresh turmeric, peeled

2 g (⅛ oz) makrut lime leaves

30 g (1 oz) lemongrass, white part only, chopped

5 g (⅛ oz) candlenuts (substitute with macadamia nuts)

To make the spice paste, blend all the spice paste ingredients in a high-speed blender until smooth. Add some water to get it going, if required.

Heat a wok over medium heat then add the oil. Fry the spice paste until fragrant – this should take between 5–7 minutes.

Add the squid, lime juice and salt and toss to coat in the sambal for 1 minute.

Add the tomato sauce and sugar. Mix until the squid is fully coated in the sauce.

Serve with rice and lime to squeeze over.

Tip: Prepare the spice paste up to a day ahead and store in a clean, sterile airtight container in the refrigerator.

Warning: Candlenuts are toxic if consumed raw or undercooked.

ORH CHIEN
Oyster omelette

Orh chien is a classic hawker stall dish. Very popular in the North of Malaysia in Penang, and often cooked over charcoal. Smaller oysters are best for this omelette. The tapioca and rice flours in the batter give it a chewy texture and when fried turn crispy.

SERVES 2
PREPARATION TIME 15 minutes
COOKING TIME 10 minutes

2 tablespoons neutral-flavoured cooking oil

4 × 70 g (2½ oz) eggs, beaten

240 g (8½ oz) oysters (about 8–10 oysters)

2 teaspoons fish sauce

1 teaspoon light soy sauce

20 g (¾ oz) dried chilli paste (chilli boh)

10 g (¼ oz) each of chopped spring onions (scallions) and coriander (cilantro) leaves

BATTER

30 g (1 oz) tapioca flour

2 teaspoons rice flour

pinch of salt

CHILLI SAUCE

40 g (1½ oz) garlic

100 g (3½ oz) long red chillies, seeded and roughly chopped

2 tablespoons white vinegar

20 g (¾ oz) white sugar

salt, to taste

Start by making the chilli sauce. Blend all the sauce ingredients together until smooth.

To make the batter, combine all the batter ingredients with 125 ml (4 fl oz/½ cup) water in a jug or bowl.

Heat a wok over high heat then add the oil. Gradually pour in the batter. Cook until the edges start to crisp up – this should take about 3 minutes. (You want the batter to be crispy but not burnt.)

Add the eggs and mix to cook slightly for 10 seconds. Add the oysters, fish sauce, soy sauce and chilli paste. Fry for a couple of minutes before adding the spring onions and coriander.

Serve the omelette hot with the chilli sauce.

DEEP-FRIED CRISPY OYSTERS

Deep-fried oysters are like an explosion in your mouth. The crisp batter works beautifully with the creaminess of the just-cooked oysters.

SERVES 4

PREPARATION TIME 10 minutes
(+ 10 minutes draining)

COOKING TIME 10 minutes

450 g (1 lb) shucked oysters

neutral-flavoured cooking oil, for deep-frying

50 g (1¾ oz/⅓ cup) plain (all-purpose) flour

shredded iceberg lettuce to serve

thinly sliced red chilli to garnish

any chilli sauce to serve

BATTER

110 g (¾ cup) plain (all-purpose) flour

½ teaspoon baking powder

½ teaspoon salt

⅛ teaspoon ground white pepper

⅛ teaspoon garlic powder

⅛ teaspoon onion powder

160 ml (5½ fl oz/⅔ cup) ice-cold sparkling or soda water

½ teaspoon sesame oil

Drain the oysters from the container and rinse them with cold water. (Be careful when you handle the oysters as they are quite delicate.) Drain the oysters in a strainer for at least 10 minutes.

Mix the flour, baking powder, salt, pepper, garlic powder and onion powder for the batter in a bowl until combined.

Heat the oil in a wok over a medium-high heat. To test if the oil is hot enough, put a wooden chopstick in the oil. If you see tiny bubbles gather around it, the oil is ready. (Alternatively, use a thermometer. It should register between 170–180°C/340–360°F.)

Just before you're ready to deep-fry the oysters, add the sparkling or soda water to the batter mixture. (This will make the oysters crispier.) Mix until smooth then add the sesame oil.

Lightly pat dry each oyster with a paper towel then coat each oyster lightly with the flour until evenly coated.

Dip each oyster into the batter until completely coated then carefully lift out of the batter.

To deep-fry the oysters, you must check the temperature of the oil to ensure it's maintained at 170–180°C (340–360°F). The oil will cool quickly as you add the oysters then heat up once they start cooking. To avoid the oysters sticking to the bottom of the wok, lower the oysters halfway into the oil in batches using tongs or a slotted spoon (do not overcrowd the wok). Slowly move them around for a few seconds to cook the batter a little then drop them completely into the oil. Once they are golden in colour, use tongs or a slotted spoon to lift the oysters out and drain them on a metal cooling rack.

Scatter lettuce over a serving dish. Top with the crispy oysters and chilli. Serve with chilli sauce.

FRIED LALA *WITH* TAUCU

Fried pipis with soybean paste

These pipis came from Goolwa in South Australia. Pipis are a super versatile mollusc that pair well with pasta, served with a sauce and bread or a quick fry like this. They take no time to cook and impart a sweet and nutty flavour.

SERVES 6

PREPARATION TIME 10 minutes

COOKING TIME 10 minutes

500 g (1 lb 2 oz) lala (clams or pipis)

2 tablespoons neutral-flavoured cooking oil

20 g (¾ oz) red chillies, finely chopped

30 g (1 oz) garlic, crushed

30 g (1 oz) piece fresh ginger, julienned

60 g (2 oz) red Asian shallots, finely diced

30 g (1 oz) fermented soybean paste (taucu)

1 tablespoon oyster sauce

1 teaspoon white sugar

chopped herb leaves to garnish

Wash the lala thoroughly with water then repeat 2–3 times to remove any sand in the shell itself.

Heat the oil in a wok over medium-high heat. Fry the chillies, garlic, ginger and shallots for 30 seconds until fragrant.

Add the soybean paste, oyster sauce, sugar and 250 ml (8½ fl oz/1 cup) water and bring to the boil. As soon as the sauce is bubbling, add the lala. Cover the wok with a domed lid and cook for 2–3 minutes until the lala open up.

Serve immediately in a serving bowl, garnished with some herbs.

PAK CHEOK HAR

Cantonese boiled prawns

Pak cheok har is easy to master and brings out the best of flavours when you have freshly caught prawns.

SERVES 6
PREPARATION TIME 15 minutes
COOKING TIME 10 minutes

60 g (2 oz) piece
fresh ginger, sliced

500 g (1 lb 2 oz)
raw tiger prawns,
deveined, legs and
whiskers trimmed,
and tip of the head
removed

salt to taste

DIPPING SAUCE

2 tablespoons
neutral-flavoured
cooking oil

10 g (¼ oz) piece
fresh ginger, grated

10 g (¼ oz) garlic,
grated

60 ml (2 fl oz/¼ cup)
light soy sauce

1 teaspoon caster
(superfine) sugar

1 teaspoon salt

thinly sliced spring
onions (scallions)
to garnish

To make the dipping sauce, heat a wok over low heat then add the oil. Add the grated ginger and garlic and fry until fragrant – this should take 60–90 seconds. Add the soy sauce, sugar, salt and 2 tablespoons water. Continue to stir until the sugar has dissolved. Transfer the sauce to a ramekin.

Fill the clean wok with water (enough to submerge the prawns in). Add the sliced ginger and season with salt. Bring to the boil over high heat then add the prawns and boil for 2–3 minutes until just cooked. Remove the prawns with a slotted spoon and drain. Transfer to a serving dish. Discard the water.

Transfer the prawns to a serving plate and sprinkle with spring onions. Serve with the dipping sauce.

BUTTER PRAWNS *WITH* EGG FLOSS

Butter prawns with egg floss doesn't only taste good, it's also very textural and has a good amount of crunch. The creamy taste of butter with the sweet and salty flavoured egg floss, in addition to the crispy prawns makes this dish simply irresistible and totally addictive.

SERVES 6
PREPARATION TIME 20 minutes
COOKING TIME 15 minutes

500 g (1 lb 2 oz) raw large tiger prawns (shrimp)

60 g (2 oz/ ½ cup) cornflour (cornstarch)

1 teaspoon salt

neutral-flavoured cooking oil, for deep-frying

60 g (2 oz) garlic, crushed

20 g (¾ oz) bird's eye chillies, sliced finely

20 g (¾ oz) curry leaves

40 g (1½ oz) caster (superfine) sugar

2 teaspoons chicken stock (bouillon) powder

EGG FLOSS

240 g (8½ oz) egg yolks (from about 4 eggs), lightly beaten

200 g (8 oz) butter or margarine

200 ml (7 fl oz) neutral-flavoured cooking oil

First, clean the prawns. Using sharp kitchen scissors, first cut the rostrum (the sharp spine above the prawn head). Then trim off the sharp top of the head, the whiskers and legs. Next, cut off the telson (the sharp point on the tail). Using a toothpick, prick into the middle to devein the prawns. Rinse the prawns under cold running water. Drain and pat dry with paper towel.

Put the prawns in a large bowl. Toss with the cornflour and salt.

Heat the oil in a wok over medium-high heat. To test if the oil is hot enough, put a wooden chopstick in the oil. If you see tiny bubbles gather around it, the oil is ready. (Alternatively, use a thermometer. It should register between 170–180°C/340–360°F.)

Dust off the excess cornflour mixture and gently add the coated prawns to the wok. Cook for 2–3 minutes on one side until cooked through and golden. Drain on paper towel.

Let the oil heat back up and fry the prawns again for 2–3 minutes, turning halfway through. Drain the prawns, reserving the excess oil in a jug or bowl. Clean the wok.

To make the egg floss, strain the egg yolks over a sieve into a measuring cup to get a smooth mixture. Return the wok to medium-low heat and add the butter and oil. Once the butter has melted, drizzle the egg yolk in one steady stream while using a whisk to stir vigorously, creating fine ribbons of egg floss.

Turn the heat to low and use a wok spatula to fry the egg floss until the oil starts to become foamy. Add the garlic, chillies, curry leaves, sugar and stock powder and stir until combined.

Add the fried prawns and toss through to coat. Serve immediately.

CEREAL PRAWNS

Cereal prawns are buttery, milky and super-fragrant, and popular in Malaysia and Singapore at many zi char (wok cooking) restaurants. The cereal referred to is Nestlé Nestum, which is a key ingredient for this dish. The prawns are sweet, juicy and tender, while the cereal coating adds a delightful crunchiness and a hint of sweetness. The aromatic curry leaves infuse a distinctly South-East Asian essence, while the chilli provides a gentle kick of spice. The buttery richness ties all the elements together.

SERVES 6
PREPARATION TIME 20 minutes
COOKING TIME 20 minutes

300 g (10½ oz) raw large tiger prawns (shrimp)

2 × 70 g (2½ oz) eggs

50 g (1¾ oz/ ⅓ cup) plain (all-purpose) flour

50 g (1¾ oz) cornflour (cornstarch)

pinch of salt and ground white pepper

neutral-flavoured cooking oil, for deep-frying, plus extra 2 tablespoons

150 g (5½ oz) butter

10 g (¼ oz) bird's eye chillies, finely chopped

10 g (¼ oz) curry leaves

CEREAL COATING

250 g (9 oz) Nestlé Nestum cereal (substitute with oat flakes)

2 tablespoons milk powder

1 tablespoon caster (superfine) sugar

pinch of salt and ground white pepper

Using sharp kitchen scissors or a sharp knife, make a slit along the middle of the back to expose the dark vein. Using a toothpick, prick into the middle to devein the prawns. Leave the shells intact. Rinse the prawns under cold running water. Drain and pat dry with paper towel

Beat the eggs in a bowl. Add the flour, cornflour, salt and pepper.

Heat the oil in a wok over medium-high heat. To test if the oil is hot enough, put a wooden chopstick in the oil. If you see tiny bubbles gather around it, the oil is ready. (Alternatively, use a thermometer. It should register between 170–180°C/340–360°F.)

Deep-fry the prawns, turning, for about 2–3 minutes until bright red and flesh is opaque. Drain on paper towel.

Discard the excess oil and clean the wok.

To make the cereal coating, combine the coating ingredients in a bowl.

Melt the butter in the wok. Add the extra oil to prevent the butter from burning. Fry the chillies and curry leaves for 30 seconds before adding in the cereal coating. Toss quickly then add the prawns and toss until coated. Serve immediately.

HAR LOK
Fried prawns with a sticky sauce

Har lok is a Cantonese-style fried prawn dish with a sticky sweet and sour glaze flavoured with aromatics. It's East meets West using a mix of Asian and Western sauces. The prawns are cooked in their shell to impart extra flavour and seal in all the sauce. These beautiful tiger prawns are from Western Australia.

SERVES 6–8

PREPARATION TIME 15 minutes

10 raw large prawns (shrimp) (I used Skull Island tigers, but you can substitute with any prawns you prefer), deveined and whiskers removed, leaving the tails intact

neutral-flavoured cooking oil, for deep-frying

20 g (¾ oz) piece fresh ginger, julienned

30 g (1 oz) red Asian shallots, finely sliced

10 g (¼ oz) garlic, crushed

10 g (¼ oz) bird's eye chillies, finely chopped

salt and ground white pepper to taste

chopped herb leaves to garnish

SAUCE

20 g (¾ oz) tamarind puree

1 tablespoon soy sauce

2 tablespoons oyster sauce

2 tablespoons dark cooking caramel (black soy sauce)

2 teaspoons Worcestershire sauce

2 teaspoons caster (superfine) sugar

Season the cleaned prawns. Set aside.

Heat the oil in a wok over medium-high heat. To test if the oil is hot enough, put a wooden chopstick in the oil. If you see tiny bubbles gather around it, the oil is ready. (Alternatively, use a thermometer. It should register between 170–180°C/340–360°F.)

In batches, add the prawns and fry until nearly cooked through. (The prawns will turn to a bright red colour when they are cooked.) Drain on paper towel.

Meanwhile, make the sauce. Combine all the sauce ingredients in a jug.

Discard the excess oil from the wok, leaving about 2 tablespoons of oil in the wok. Return the wok to medium heat and fry the ginger, shallots, garlic and chillies until fragrant. Add the prawns followed by the sauce. Toss to coat the prawns.

To serve, place on a large serving dish and garnish with some herbs.

TEOCHEW STEAMED FISH

A steamed fish with light flavours is the best way to cook fish when you have fresh fish like this gorgeous coral trout. Of course you can use any other white fish you like, but one that has a firm but sweet flesh and is non-oily works best for this method of cooking.

The reason it is called Teochew steamed fish is because it was made popular by the Swa tow people who worked a lot as fishermen or as boatmen.

SERVES 6

PREPARATION TIME 15 minutes

COOKING TIME 20 minutes

750 g (1 lb 11 oz) whole coral trout (substitute with any white fish of your choice), cleaned and gutted

30 g (1 oz) piece fresh ginger, julienned, plus extra, julienned, for topping the fish (use young ginger if available)

30 g (1 oz) salted plums (umeboshi), pitted and halved

50 g (1¾ oz) preserved mustard greens, rinsed and cut into 2 cm (¾ in) lengths

100 g (3½ oz) silken tofu, cut into 2 cm (¾ in) cubes

30 g (1 oz) tomato, quartered

20 g (¾ oz) dried shiitake mushrooms, rehydrated in hot water for 30 minutes, drained and sliced

2 teaspoons fish sauce

1 tablespoon light soy sauce

1 tablespoon shaoxing rice wine

salt, to taste

shredded spring onions (scallions) to garnish

Fill a wok with water until 5 cm (2 in) deep. Put a trivet in the middle of the wok. Cover the wok with a domed lid and bring the water to a rapid boil over high heat.

Make 2 deep incisions diagonally at about a 30° angle on both sides of the fish. Lightly salt the outside and in the cavity of the fish.

Put some ginger and plum in the cuts and in the cavity. Put the mustard greens and remaining ginger and plum on a heatproof plate or metal tray that fits in the wok. Lay the fish on top. Scatter the tofu, tomato and mushrooms around the fish and top with extra ginger. Drizzle the fish sauce, soy sauce and shaoxing over the fish.

Carefully lower the plate or tray onto the trivet and steam the fish for about 10 minutes until internal temperature reaches 63°C (145°F) at the thickest part. Remove from the heat.

Top with spring onions and serve immediately.

FISH HEAD CURRY

Fish head curry is a popular dish in Malaysia and Singapore that is a hybrid between both Indian and Chinese ethnicities. This unique dish combines the use of fish heads, which were often discarded, served with a complex and aromatic curry sauce.

SERVES 6

PREPARATION TIME 20 minutes

COOKING TIME 40 minutes

750–850 g (1 lb 11 oz–1 lb 14 oz) fish head/s (such as garoupa, red emperor or red snapper), cleaned, cut into halves and seasoned with salt

3 tablespoons neutral-flavoured cooking oil

½ teaspoon mustard seeds

30 g (1 oz) brown onion, sliced thinly

2 g (⅛ oz) curry leaves

10 g (¼ oz) lemongrass, cut in half lengthways and bruised lightly

100 g (3½ oz) tamarind puree

30 g (1 oz) long thin eggplant (aubergine), sliced

60 g (2 oz) ripe tomato, quartered

200 g (8 oz) okra

10 g (¼ oz) red chillies, seeded and halved

5 g (⅛ oz) green chillies, seeded and halved

250 ml (8½ fl oz/ 1 cup) coconut milk

salt and white sugar to taste

coriander (cilantro) leaves to garnish

CURRY PASTE

2 tablespoons fish curry powder

10 g (¼ oz) chilli paste

10 g (¼ oz) belacan (shrimp paste), ground with a mortar and pestle

Heat a wok over a high heat then add 1 litre (34 fl oz/4 cups) water. Bring to the boil then add the fish head/s and cook until almost cooked through. Remove the fish head/s and set aside. Reserve the liquid in a jug.

Heat the clean wok over a high heat then add the oil. Fry the mustard seeds until they pop. Add the curry paste ingredients and fry until fragrant. Add the onion, curry leaves and lemongrass and cook for a further 5 minutes until the onion have softened.

Return the reserved liquid to the wok and bring to a simmer. Add the tamarind, eggplant, tomato, okra and chillies. Cover the wok with a domed lid and simmer for 15 minutes.

Once the vegetables are tender, add the reserved fish head/s back in and simmer for a further 5–7 minutes until cooked through. Season with salt and sugar. Pour in the coconut milk.

Gently dish out onto a large serving dish and garnish with some coriander.

ASSAM PEDAS

Tamarind fish

Assam pedas is a dish widely cooked in Malay and Nyonya cultures. It is believed to originate from West Sumatra. However, it is incredibly popular in the Malay culture. Assam means tamarind and pedas means spicy or hot. One of the key ingredients of the dish is fresh daun kesum (Vietnamese mint) and lots of it. It imparts a beautiful fragrance paired with the sourness from the tamarind. The other ingredients that are imperative are the tamarind and okra. My mum would make her version for us frequently when we were growing up. This is her recipe, which I have tweaked slightly.

SERVES 6

PREPARATION TIME 30 minutes
(+ 5 minutes cooling)

COOKING TIME 40 minutes

200 ml (7 fl oz) neutral-flavoured cooking oil, plus extra for the spice paste

100 g (3½ oz) tomato, quartered

130 g (4½ oz) tamarind puree

60 g (2 oz) caster (superfine) sugar

60 g (2 oz) torch ginger flower (bunga kantan) (optional), halved lengthways, plus extra, thinly sliced, to garnish (find in Asian supermarket freezers)

30 g (1 oz) Vietnamese mint, plus extra, shredded, to garnish

1 kg (2 lb 3 oz) white fish of choice (such as snapper, sea bass or stingray. You can use the whole fish, but I use deboned fillets)

80 g (2¾ oz) okra

2 teaspoons salt

steamed jasmine rice to serve

SPICE PASTE

50 g (1¾ oz) dried red chillies, seeded, rehydrated in hot water for 15 minutes and drained

100 g (3½ oz) long red chillies, seeded and chopped

30 g (1 oz) garlic

60 g (2 oz) red Asian shallots, chopped

30 g (1 oz) piece fresh turmeric, peeled and chopped

60 g (2 oz) fresh lemongrass stem, white part only, chopped

4 teaspoons belacan (shrimp paste), toasted (see tip on page 97)

Start by making the spice paste. Put all the spice paste ingredients in a high-speed blender and blend until smooth. Add some extra oil to help blend.

Heat a wok over a medium-high heat then add the oil. Cook the spice paste, stirring constantly, for 5 minutes until fragrant. (You will start to notice the oil splitting from the paste as the colour of the paste deepens. That's when you know it's ready.)

Add the tomato and allow to soften, about 5 minutes. Add the tamarind, sugar, ginger flower, if using, mint and 1 litre (34 fl oz/4 cups) water. Cover with a domed lid and simmer over a low heat for 20 minutes.

Add the fish and cook for a further 8 minutes or until the fish is nearly cooked through. Add the okra and salt. (The flavour you are looking for is predominantly sour with a hint of sweetness.)

Remove from the heat and allow to cool on the stove for 5 minutes. Serve with rice and garnish with some extra mint and ginger flower, if using.

Tip: Prepare the spice paste up to a day ahead and store in a clean, sterile, airtight container in the refrigerator.

HU PAO
Nyonya fish parcels

Pronounced 'who pow', hu pao is a Nyonya version of steamed otak-otak, which is a spiced fish parcel wrapped in banana leaves. My uncle often makes this dish for us over Chinese New Year. It is so delicately spiced with beautiful aromas of fragrant herbs.

SERVES 6

PREPARATION TIME 30 minutes

COOKING TIME 12 minutes

500 g (1 lb 2 oz) skinless barramundi fillets

500 g (1 lb 2 oz) banana leaves

50 g (1¾ oz) betel leaves, stems removed

SPICE PASTE

10 g (¼ oz) candlenuts (substitute with macadamia nuts)

30 g (1 oz) piece fresh galangal

10 g (¼ oz) lemongrass stem, outer skin removed and white part sliced

10 g (¼ oz) piece fresh turmeric

100 g (3½ oz) red Asian shallots

4 teaspoons belacan (shrimp paste), toasted (see tip on page 97)

30 g (1 oz) fresh red chillies, chopped

10 g (¼ oz) dried red chillies, rehydrated in warm water for 10 minutes and drained

CUSTARD

2 × 70 g (2½ oz) eggs

250 ml (8½ fl oz/ 1 cup) coconut milk

2 tablespoons rice flour

4 makrut lime leaves, thinly sliced

pinch of ground white pepper

salt and sugar to taste

Start by preparing the spice paste. Blend all the spice paste ingredients in a high-speed blender until smooth. Add a tablespoon of water to get it going, if required.

Combine the custard ingredients in a bowl then add the spice paste.

Cut the fish into 6 equal portions then add to custard mixture and stir to coat then set aside to marinate.

Meanwhile, prepare your banana leaves by cutting them into 6 × 20 cm (8 in) squares. Hold each leaf over an open flame until wilted. (This makes them easier to fold. I use the flames from the stove to do this, holding them with a pair of tongs.)

To assemble the parcels, lay a wilted banana leaf square on a flat surface and put the fish in the centre. Place 2 betel leaves on top of the fish. Bring 2 opposite sides of the banana leaf together in the centre then fold over the other opposite sides to form a triangular-shaped parcel, securing with a toothpick.

Fill a wok with water until 7.5 cm (3 in) deep. Put a trivet in the middle of the wok. Heat over a high heat. Place the parcels on a heatproof plate or metal tray that fits in the wok and carefully lower onto the trivet. Cover with a domed lid and steam until the fish is cooked and the custard sets – this should take about 10 minutes.

Tip: Prepare the spice paste up to a day ahead and store in a clean, sterile, airtight container in the refrigerator.

Warning: Candlenuts are toxic if consumed raw or undercooked.

IKAN REMPAH

Spiced fish

It is not uncommon to find different variations of ikan rempah and it all comes down to the rempah (spice paste) that you use. You can add everything from shallots to chillies to turmeric to lemongrass. The use of the rempah is to mask the strong flavour of smaller fish, such as sardines or mackerel.

SERVES 6

PREPARATION TIME 15 minutes (+ cooling)

COOKING TIME 15 minutes

200 ml (7 fl oz) neutral-flavoured cooking oil, plus extra for frying

500 g (1 lb 2 oz) sardines (substitute with any oily fish)

salt to taste

your favourite sambal to serve (see Sauces chapter on page 20)

halved limes or lemons to serve

1 tablespoon tamarind purée to garnish

SPICE PASTE

200 g (7 oz) dried red chillies, seeded, rehydrated in hot water for 15 minutes and drained

60 g (2 oz) red onions, chopped

30 g (1 oz) garlic

70 g (2½ oz) lemongrass stems, white part only, chopped

30 g (1 oz) piece fresh galangal, sliced

10 g (¼ oz) piece fresh turmeric, sliced

Start with the spice paste. Blend all the spice paste ingredients in a high-speed blender until smooth. Add a tablespoon of water to get it going, if required.

Heat a wok over a medium-high heat then add the oil. Fry the spice paste for 5 minutes until fragrant. Pour in 125 ml (4 fl oz/½ cup) water and cook until thickened. Remove from the heat and set aside to cool.

Meanwhile, gut and clean the fish. Make an incision across the belly lengthways to create a pocket. Stuff each fish belly with the spice paste mixture then coat the entire fish as well.

In a clean wok over a medium heat add a drizzle of extra oil and fry the fish in batches, for 3 minutes each side until cooked through (flesh will be opaque and flaky). Drizzle in extra oil between batches, if required.

Serve the fish with sambal and limes or lemons to squeeze over.

Tip: Prepare the spice paste up to a day ahead and store in a clean, sterile, airtight container in the refrigerator.

07

VEGETABLES

ACHAR
Malaysian pickles

Achar is a Malaysian pickle consisting of various kinds of vegetables and fruits. The pickling liquid is made with a blend of spices and aromatics, vinegar and sugar. You will often find peanuts and sesame seeds in achar as well.

MAKES 1 kg (2 lb 3 oz) or 2 jars
PREPARATION TIME 45 minutes
(+ 30 minutes standing & cooling)
COOKING TIME 20 minutes

1 small head (about 300 g/10½ oz) cauliflower, cut into small florets

150 g (5½ oz) Lebanese (short) cucumbers, cut into 8 cm (3¼ in) batons

½ small head (about 200 g/7 oz) white cabbage

100 g (3½ oz) carrots, cut into 8 cm (3¼ in) batons

20 g (¾ oz) long red chillies, cut into strips

60 ml (2 fl oz/¼ cup) neutral-flavoured cooking oil

100 ml (3½ fl oz) rice wine vinegar or white vinegar

40 g (1½ oz) caster (superfine) sugar

200 g (7 oz) peeled pineapple, cut into small bite-sized pieces

60 g (2 oz) toasted crushed peanuts

1 teaspoon toasted sesame seeds

salt to taste

SPICE PASTE

120 g (4½ oz) red Asian shallots, roughly chopped

20 g (¾ oz) long red chillies

20 g (¾ oz) piece fresh turmeric (substitute with ½ teaspoon ground turmeric)

5 g (⅛ oz) candlenuts (substitute with macadamia nuts)

Put the cauliflower, cucumbers, cabbage, carrots and chillies in a colander and sprinkle over some salt. Allow to sit for 20–30 minutes to remove any excess liquid. Rinse and drain.

To make the spice paste, blend all the spice paste ingredients with 2 tablespoons water in a high-speed blender until smooth.

Heat a wok over a high heat then add the oil. Fry the spice paste for 2–3 minutes until fragrant. Pour in the vinegar and 500 ml (17 fl oz/ 2 cups) water and bring to the boil. Add the sugar and season with salt. Add the vegetables and pineapple, turn the heat to low and simmer in the sauce for 15 minutes.

Add the peanuts and sesame seeds and mix to combine. Once the vegetables have softened, remove from the heat and allow to cool completely.

Tip: Store the vegetables with the pickling liquid in clean, sterile, airtight containers or jars in the refrigerator for up to 4 weeks. The flavour intensifies day by day.

Warning: Candlenuts are toxic if consumed raw or undercooked.

SAYUR URAP

Steamed vegetables with spiced grated coconut

Urap is a salad dish of steamed vegetables mixed with seasoned and spiced grated coconut known as serundeng that originated from Java, Indonesia. I love having Sayur urap as a side dish to Beef rendang or Ayam masak merah.

SERVES 6 (as a side)
PREPARATION TIME 10 minutes
COOKING TIME 5 minutes

200 g (7 oz) snake (yard-long) beans, cut into 5 cm (2 in) lengths

100 g (3½ oz) bean sprouts

150 g (5½ oz) morning glory (kangkung), cut into 5 cm (2 in) lengths

50 g (1¾ oz) English spinach, roots removed

200 g (7 oz) Serundeng (coconut floss, see recipe on page 40)

salt to taste

Fill a wok with water (enough to blanch the vegetables in). Fill a bowl with ice-cold water. Place the wok over a medium heat and bring to the boil. Season heavily with salt. Blanch the vegetables, starting with the beans for 1 minute followed by the bean sprouts, morning glory and English spinach for 20–30 seconds. Transfer the vegetables to the ice-cold water to stop them cooking further. Drain.

To serve, scatter the vegetables on a serving platter and top with the Serundeng.

SILKEN TOFU *WITH* CARAMELISED SHALLOTS

I have fond memories of my mum making this for us as kids. It is a simple dish yet packed full of flavour.

SERVES 4 (as a side)
PREPARATION TIME 15 minutes
COOKING TIME 20 minutes

1 × 300 g (10½ oz) block silken tofu

1 teaspoon sesame oil

thinly sliced spring onions (scallions) to garnish

fried ginger floss to garnish (see tip)

steamed jasmine rice to serve

CARAMELISED SHALLOTS

neutral-flavoured cooking oil, for frying

40 g (1½ oz) red Asian shallots, thinly sliced

1 tablespoon dark cooking caramel (substitute with kecap manis)

1 tablespoon light soy sauce

2 teaspoons caster (superfine) sugar

Place the tofu on a heatproof serving dish. Place the dish on a trivet in a wok. Fill the wok with enough water to come up to just under the dish. Place the wok over a high heat. Steam, covered, for 8–10 minutes then remove from the heat.

Meanwhile, make the caramelised shallots. Heat a small frying pan over a medium heat then add the cooking oil. Fry the shallots for 5–7 minutes. Add the caramel, soy sauce and sugar and cook until caramelised.

Spoon the caramelised shallots over the tofu then drizzle over the sesame oil. Garnish with some spring onions and ginger floss. Serve with rice.

Tip: To make ginger floss, thinly julienne fresh ginger and deep-fry in hot oil for 30–60 seconds until golden. Drain on paper towel.

FRIED GREEN BEANS *AND* MINCED PORK

Fried green beans and minced pork is a classic Chinese restaurant dish. You can mix up the toppings by using a different kind of minced (ground) meat or mushrooms.

SERVES 6 (as a side)
PREPARATION TIME 10 minutes
COOKING TIME 15 minutes

neutral-flavoured cooking oil, for deep-frying

500 g (1 lb 2 oz) green beans, trimmed and strings removed

100 g (3½ oz) minced (ground) pork

10 g (¼ oz) piece fresh ginger, grated

1 teaspoon white sugar

½ teaspoon salt

1 tablespoon light soy sauce

1 tablespoon oyster sauce

2 teaspoons shaoxing rice wine

Heat the oil in a wok over a medium-high heat. To test if the oil is hot enough, put a wooden chopstick in the oil. If you see tiny bubbles gather around it, the oil is ready. (Alternatively, use a thermometer. It should register between 170–180°C/340–360°F.)

Deep-fry the beans until wrinkled. Drain on paper towel then gently arrange on a serving dish.

Drain the excess oil from the wok, leaving about 2 tablespoons of oil in the wok. Return the wok to a high heat and add the pork, ginger, sugar and salt and fry for 30 seconds.

Pour in the soy sauce, oyster sauce, shaoxing and 75 ml (2½ fl oz) water and cook until the liquid reduces by half. Remove from the heat.

Spoon the pork mixture over the beans to serve.

FRIED LETTUCE *WITH* OYSTER SAUCE *AND* GARLIC

Many people will overlook the versatility of the humble lettuce and often only use it in its raw form in a salad. I think when lettuce is fried and slightly charred it imparts a gentle sweetness while still retaining its crunch.

SERVES 4 (as a side)
PREPARATION TIME 15 minutes
COOKING TIME 5 minutes

250 g (9 oz) cos (romaine) lettuce

3 tablespoons neutral-flavoured cooking oil

20 g (¾ oz) garlic, crushed

1 tablespoon light soy sauce

1 tablespoon oyster sauce (omit for vegetarian)

steamed jasmine rice to serve

Start by preparing the romaine lettuce. Separate into individual leaves. Wash the leaves clean, especially the base where they store more dirt. Drain.

Fill a wok with 750 ml (25½ fl oz/3 cups) water. Bring to the boil over a high heat. Add 1 tablespoon of the oil and the lettuce. Cook for about 20 seconds until just wilted. Immediately scoop them out and drain. Arrange them on a serving plate.

Drain the water from the wok and immediately return the wok to a high heat. Add the remaining oil and fry the garlic. Pour in the soy sauce, oyster sauce and 3 tablespoons water. Bring to a simmer then remove from the heat. Pour the sauce over the lettuce.

Serve immediately with rice.

FRIED BITTER GOURD *WITH* EGG

Bitter gourd (bitter melon) is one of those controversial vegetables. You either love it or hate it. I love it and don't actually mind the bitter flavour. It's also high in vitamins A and C. My tip is to salt the bitter gourd before using to remove the bitterness.

SERVES 6 (as a side)
PREPARATION TIME 15 minutes
COOKING TIME 10 minutes

2 × 250 g (9 oz) bitter gourds (bitter melon)

5 × 70 g (2½ oz) eggs

1 teaspoon sesame oil

pinch of salt and ground white pepper

3 tablespoons neutral-flavoured cooking oil

1 tablespoon shaoxing rice wine

2 teaspoons light soy sauce

1 tablespoon oyster sauce (omit for vegetarian)

½ teaspoon white sugar

Cut each bitter gourd in half lengthways. Using a spoon, scoop out the seeds and scrape the inside clean of any white pith. Cut the bitter gourd into very thin slices.

Pour 750 ml (25½ fl oz/3 cups) water into a wok and season liberally with salt. Bring to the boil over a high heat then blanch the bitter gourd for 30 seconds until slightly softened. Drain.

Beat the eggs with the sesame oil and a pinch of salt and white pepper in a bowl.

Return the clean wok to a high heat until at smoking point. Add 2 tablespoons of the cooking oil followed immediately by the egg mixture. Scramble the eggs quickly so they remain tender and not browned. When the eggs are almost cooked, transfer to a bowl.

Add the remaining cooking oil to the wok then fry the bitter gourd for 30 seconds. Add the shaoxing around the perimeter of the wok. Stir-fry for another 30 seconds then add the soy sauce, oyster sauce and sugar.

Return the scrambled eggs to the wok and mix until just cooked through. Remove from the heat. Transfer to a serving dish.

Serve immediately.

FISH-FRAGRANT FRIED EGGPLANT

Fish-fragrant eggplant has got absolutely nothing to do with fish! Folklore has it that the dish was originally served with river fish and the leftover sauce was used to cook the eggplant.

SERVES 4 (as a side)
PREPARATION TIME 15 minutes
(+ 30 minutes standing)
COOKING TIME 10 minutes

300 g (10½ oz) long thin eggplant (aubergine)

60 ml (2 fl oz/¼ cup) neutral-flavoured cooking oil

10 g (¼ oz) dried red chillies, rehydrated in warm water for 15 minutes and drained

10 g (¼ oz) garlic, crushed

10 g (¼ oz) piece fresh ginger, julienned

1 red Asian shallot, thinly sliced

salt and ground white pepper to taste

steamed jasmine rice to serve

finely sliced spring onions (scallions) to garnish

SAUCE

1 tablespoon oyster sauce (omit for vegetarian)

2 tablespoons light soy sauce

1 tablespoon shaoxing rice wine

2 teaspoons sesame oil

1 teaspoon white sugar

Cut the eggplant diagonally into 2 cm (¾ in) slices and put in a colander. Sprinkle with salt liberally and allow to sit for at least 30 minutes. Rinse, drain and pat dry with paper towel.

To make the sauce, combine all the sauce ingredients in a jug.

Heat a wok over a high heat then add the cooking oil. Fry the chillies, garlic, ginger and shallot for 30 seconds then add the eggplant. Fry, constantly tossing, for 5 minutes until the eggplant is cooked through.

Add the sauce and stir through. Season with white pepper. Remove from the heat and transfer to a serving dish.

Garnish with spring onions and serve with rice.

SAMBAL TERUNG
Eggplant sambal

A delicious combination of soft and melt-in-your-mouth eggplant doused in a spicy gravy.

SERVES 6 (as a side)
PREPARATION TIME 20 minutes
COOKING TIME 15 minutes

500 ml (17 fl oz/
2 cups) neutral-
flavoured cooking oil

1 kg (2 lb 3 oz)
long thin eggplant
(aubergine), cut
in half lengthways
then into 5 cm (2 in)
pieces

200 ml (7 fl oz)
coconut cream

2 tablespoons white
sugar

1 teaspoon salt

makrut lime leaves
to serve

KERISIK (COCONUT BUTTER)

500 g (1 lb 2 oz)
desiccated
(shredded) coconut

SPICE PASTE

10 g (¼ oz) dried
red chillies, seeded,
rehydrated in hot
water for 10 minutes
and drained

200 g (7 oz)
dried baby shrimp
(substitute with
cashew nuts for
vegetarian)

100 g (3½ oz)
red Asian shallots,
chopped

50 g (1¾ oz) garlic

60 g (2 oz) piece
fresh ginger, peeled
and chopped

20 g (¾ oz) piece
fresh turmeric,
peeled and chopped

5 g (⅛ oz) fennel
seeds

5 g (⅛ oz) coriander
seeds

Start by making the kerisik. Toast the coconut in a wok over a low–medium heat until golden. Transfer to a high-speed blender and blend until a buttery consistency.

Return the clean wok to a high heat then add the oil. Fry the eggplant, turning, until tender. Remove from the heat and drain on paper towel. Reserve the oil.

To make the spice paste, blend all the spice paste ingredients in a high-speed blender until smooth. Add some extra oil or water to help blend, if required.

Return the wok with the reserved oil to a medium heat. Fry the spice paste until fragrant, about 5 minutes. Reduce the heat to low and add the kerisik. Mix until evenly combined.

Pour in the coconut cream and stir through. Bring to the boil then add the sugar and salt. Add the eggplant, toss to coat in the sauce then remove from the heat.

Place on a serving dish, add some makrut lime leaves and serve with rice.

YIN YANG KAI LAN

*Chinese broccoli
cooked two ways*

Cooking kai lan this way really showcases the versatility of the vegetable. Deep-frying the leaves makes them really crispy and resemble seaweed while the stems stay crunchy and fresh.

SERVES 6 (as a side)
PREPARATION TIME 20 minutes
COOKING TIME 10 minutes

500 g (1 lb 2 oz)
Chinese broccoli
(kai lan)

neutral-flavoured
cooking oil, for
deep-frying

30 g (1 oz) garlic,
thinly sliced

1 tablespoon light
soy sauce

1 tablespoon oyster
sauce

1 teaspoon cornflour
(cornstarch), mixed
into a slurry with
1 tablespoon water

salt, to taste

garlic chips to
garnish (see tip)

To prepare the kai lan, cut the leaves off the bunch and stack the leaves on top of each other. Roll them up and thinly slice into long ribbons. Cut the stems into 8 cm (3¼ in) lengths or to your preference.

Heat the oil in a wok over a medium-high heat. To test if the oil is hot enough, put a wooden chopstick in the oil. If you see tiny bubbles gather around it, the oil is ready. (Alternatively, use a thermometer. It should register between 170–180°C/340–360°F.)

Deep-fry the kai lan leaves for 2–3 minutes until crispy then drain on paper towel. Immediately sprinkle with some salt while the leaves are hot.

Discard the excess oil from the wok, leaving about 1 tablespoon of oil in the wok. Return the wok to a high heat and fry the garlic for 30 seconds.

Add the kai lan stems and toss. Add the soy sauce, oyster sauce and 125 ml (4 fl oz/½ cup) water and cook for 2–3 minutes until the kai lan is tender. Pour in the cornflour slurry and allow the gravy to thicken before removing from the heat.

To serve, place the stems on a serving plate, top with the leaves and garnish with some garlic chips.

Tip: To make garlic chips, thinly slice garlic and deep-fry in hot oil for 30–60 seconds until golden. Drain on paper towel.

FRIED WATERCRESS

Watercress is an incredible vegetable that can be eaten in many ways. Throw it into a salad, cook it until just wilted in a pot of hot broth or simply wok toss with garlic, ginger and soy – the delicate peppery leaves compliment the saltiness of soy sauce.

SERVES 6 (as a side)
PREPARATION TIME 5 minutes
COOKING TIME 5 minutes

60 ml (2 fl oz/¼ cup) neutral-flavoured cooking oil

20 g (¾ oz) piece fresh ginger, julienned

20 g (¾ oz) garlic, crushed

450 g (1 lb) watercress, washed thoroughly

1 teaspoon sesame oil

pinch of salt, sugar and ground white pepper

Heat the wok over a medium-high heat then add the oil. Fry the ginger for 30 seconds to flavour the oil until caramelised. (Be careful to not let it burn.) Add the garlic and stir for 15 seconds.

Add the watercress and toss for 30 seconds until it starts to wilt. Pile the watercress in the middle of the wok and cover with a domed lid, allowing it to steam for a minute.

Remove the lid and season with the sesame oil, salt, sugar and pepper. Remove from the heat.

Serve immediately.

BOK CHOY *WITH* BRAISED MUSHROOMS

This dish is simple to make and looks presentable. Soak the shiitake mushrooms and keep the liquid to use in the gravy.

SERVES 4 (as a side)
PREPARATION TIME 30 minutes
COOKING TIME 20 minutes

70 g (2½ oz) dried shiitake mushrooms, rehydrated in 750 ml (25½ fl oz/2 cups) hot water for 30 minutes and drained, liquid reserved

pinch of salt and ground white pepper

280 g (10 oz) baby bok choy (pak choy), trimmed and halved lengthways

3 tablespoons neutral-flavoured cooking oil

5 g (⅛ oz) garlic, crushed

1 tablespoon shaoxing rice wine

1 teaspoon dark cooking caramel (black soy sauce)

1 tablespoon light soy sauce

1 tablespoon oyster sauce (omit for vegetarian)

1 teaspoon sesame oil

½ teaspoon white sugar

1 teaspoon cornflour (cornstarch), mixed into a slurry with 1 tablespoon water

Remove and discard the mushroom stems.

Fill a wok with water (enough to blanch the bok choy in). Fill a bowl with ice-cold water. Place the wok over a high heat and bring to the boil. Add a pinch of salt and blanch the bok choy for 45 seconds until bright green but just wilted. Immediately remove the bok choy and dunk in the ice-cold water to stop it from cooking further. Drain and transfer to a serving plate.

Heat the clean wok over a medium-high heat then add the cooking oil. Fry the garlic and mushrooms for 15 seconds before pouring in the shaoxing.

Add the reserved mushroom liquid and bring to a simmer. Add the caramel, soy sauce, oyster sauce, sesame oil, sugar and white pepper and simmer for a further 5 minutes.

Add the cornflour slurry and stir vigorously. When the sauce thickens, remove from the heat and pour the mushrooms and gravy over the bok choy to serve.

SAMBAL TEMPEH

Tempeh is highly nutritious and a great source of protein. It's also said to help overall digestive health and is better tolerated thanks to the fermentation of the soy protein. I love having sambal tempeh as a side to complement other dishes or on its own as a snack.

SERVES 6 (as a side)
PREPARATION TIME 20 minutes (+ 10 minutes soaking)
COOKING TIME 20 minutes

100 g (3½ oz) potatoes, peeled and thinly sliced

750 ml (25½ fl oz/ 3 cups) warm water

3 teaspoons salt

neutral-flavoured cooking oil, for deep-frying, plus 1 tablespoon extra

350 g (12½ oz) organic tempeh, thinly sliced

30 g (1 oz) toasted peanuts, skin on

60 g (2 oz) red onion, thinly sliced

1 piece tamarind peel (substitute with a squeeze of lime juice)

60 g (2 oz) dried chilli paste (chilli boh)

40 g (1½ oz/¼ cup) soft brown sugar

1 long red chilli, thinly sliced

6 makrut lime leaves, thinly sliced, to garnish

Place the potatoes and warm water in a large bowl with 2 teaspoons of the salt. Soak for 10 minutes then drain and pat dry.

Meanwhile, heat the oil in a wok over a medium-high heat. To test if the oil is hot enough, put a wooden chopstick in the oil. If you see tiny bubbles gather around it, the oil is ready. (Alternatively, use a thermometer. It should register between 170–180°C/340–360°F.)

Separately deep-fry the potatoes, the tempeh and the peanuts, turning, until crispy. Remove and drain on paper towel.

Discard the oil and clean the wok. Return the wok to a high heat then add the extra oil. Fry the onion for 1 minute. Add the tamarind peel, followed by the chilli paste. Simmer, stirring occasionally, for about 2 minutes. Add the brown sugar, red chilli and remaining salt. Stir to combine.

Add the potato, tempeh and peanuts to the wok. Toss to coat thoroughly in the sambal mixture.

Transfer to a serving plate to serve. Garnish with lime leaves.

Tip: Store in a clean, sterile, airtight container in a cool, dark place for up to 1 week.

CRISPY YAM BASKET

You can add any filling you like to your yam basket. You may wish to keep it vegetarian and add tofu and vegetables or add some protein. One of my favourite combinations is with Kung pao chicken (see recipe on page 117).

SERVES 6 (as a side)
PREPARATION TIME 30 minutes (+ 5 minutes resting & 1 hour chilling)
COOKING TIME 20 minutes

300 g (10½ oz) taro, peeled and sliced

60 g (2 oz) plain (all-purpose) flour, plus extra for dusting

90 ml (3 fl oz) boiling water

½ teaspoon baking powder

½ teaspoon salt

½ teaspoon white sugar

pinch of ground white pepper

pinch of Five-spice (see recipe on page 28)

½ teaspoon sesame oil

60 g (2 oz) pork lard (substitute with melted vegetable shortening)

neutral-flavoured cooking oil, for deep-frying

35 g (1¼ oz) dried rice vermicelli

chopped coriander (cilantro) leaves to garnish

Steam the taro until tender and it tests done with a fork. Mash the taro in a large bowl.

In a separate bowl, add the flour. Slowly pour in the boiling water, stirring continuously until all the water is incorporated. When cool enough to handle, knead until a starchy paste forms. (The texture should be smooth and soft.) Set aside for 5 minutes to rest.

Add the flour mixture to the mashed taro then add the baking powder, salt, sugar, pepper, five-spice and sesame oil. Mix well to combine.

Add the lard and knead the mixture into a dough. (The dough is ready when it doesn't stick to your hands.) Divide the dough in half and wrap each portion with cling wrap. Refrigerate for 1 hour until semi-hard to make it easier to handle and shape into a ring.

Once the dough has rested, you're ready to form the ring. Sprinkle your work bench with some extra flour. Gently shape both dough portions into 1 long log then flatten. Join the 2 ends to form a ring.

Heat the cooking oil in a wok over a medium heat. (The depth of the oil has to fully cover the height of the yam basket.) To test if the oil is sufficiently hot, drop a piece of dough into the oil. If it stays at the bottom of the oil for a second before floating to the top, the oil is ready.

Add the vermicelli to the wok, then once the noodles puff up, remove immediately with a spider skimmer and set aside on a plate.

Carefully place the yam basket ring onto a large slotted spoon then fully submerge it in the hot oil. Deep-fry, increasing the heat when almost done, until golden and crispy then remove from oil. Drain and place on a serving platter.

Scatter over the fried vermicelli and top with coriander.

LO HON JAI
Buddha's delight

Buddha's Delight is a splendid vegetarian dish savoured by everyone during Chinese New Year. Traditionally eaten by saints, 'lo hon' in Chinese refers to the Sixteen Arhats (similar to the Twelve Apostles), who gained insight into the true nature of existence and have achieved nirvana. It is a significant dish in Chinese culture.

SERVES 6 (as a side)
PREPARATION TIME 15 minutes
COOKING TIME 20 minutes

15 g (½ oz) dried lily flowers

20 g (¾ oz) dried shiitake mushrooms

10 g (¼ oz) dried black fungus (wood ears)

45 g (1½ oz) dried mung bean vermicelli

neutral-flavoured cooking oil, for deep-frying

60 g (2 oz) dried bean curd sheet

20 g (¾ oz) garlic, crushed

350 g (12½ oz) Chinese cabbage (wombok), cut into 3 cm (1¼ in) lengths

2 g (⅛ oz) black moss (fat choy)

60 g (2 oz) carrots, cut into 3 mm (⅛ in) slices

120 g (4½ oz) white fermented bean curd

30 g (1 oz) white sugar

50 g (1¾ oz) bamboo shoots, cut into very thin slices

50 g (1¾ oz) baby corn

salt and ground white pepper to taste

For better presentation, tie a knot in each dried lily flower. Soak the lily flowers, shiitake, black fungus and vermicelli in lukewarm water until softened and fully rehydrated. Drain, reserving the soaking liquid.

Meanwhile, heat the oil in a wok over a medium-high heat. To test if the oil is hot enough, put a wooden chopstick in the oil. If you see tiny bubbles gather around it, the oil is ready. (Alternatively, use a thermometer. It should register between 170–180°C/340–360°F.)

Cut the bean curd sheet into smaller pieces.

Deep-fry the bean curd sheet pieces briefly, about 15-20 seconds until crispy. Remove the wok from the heat and drain the bean curd pieces on paper towel. Drain the excess oil from the wok, leaving about 2 tablespoons of oil in the wok.

Prepare the vegetables. Cut the black fungus to a similar size as the carrots. Remove the stems from the shiitake and quarter them.

Return the wok to a medium-high heat. Fry the garlic for 30 seconds to flavour the oil then add the cabbage shortly after. Stir-fry until the cabbage starts to soften.

Add the black fungus, shiitake, lily flowers, fat choy, carrots, fermented bean curd, sugar, reserved soaking liquid and 125 ml (4 fl oz/½ cup) water. Braise for 2–3 minutes.

Break the fried bean curd pieces into smaller pieces as you add them to the wok.

Add in the vermicelli, bamboo shoots and baby corn and cover the wok with a domed lid. Allow to braise for a further 5 minutes until the vegetables are softened and the sauce thickens. Season with salt and pepper. Lightly toss.

Serve immediately.

Tip: Find all the specialised ingredients for this dish at Asian grocers.

SAMBAL KANGKUNG

Morning glory cooked with sambal

When we were kids, my mum played a game where each of us were allowed to take turns to order our favourite vegetable. My brother's was snow pea sprouts fried with garlic, my sister's was fried bok choy and mine was always chilli and shrimp paste kangkung. I was always so excited when it was my turn that my siblings would often allow me to order it over theirs every now and again. Can you tell I am the youngest child? Haha!

MAKES 6 (as a side)
PREPARATION TIME 10 minutes
COOKING TIME 10 minutes

500 g (1 lb 2 oz) morning glory (kangkung)

2 tablespoons neutral-flavoured cooking oil

30 g (1 oz) red Asian shallots, halved and thinly sliced

10 g (¼ oz) garlic, crushed

60 g (2 oz) Sambal belacan (see recipe on page 36)

1 tablespoon light soy sauce

To prepare the kangkung, pick out and discard the leaves that aren't vibrant green and fresh. Cut the kangkung into 8 cm (3¼ in) lengths then rinse thoroughly in a colander under cold running water.

Heat a wok over a medium-high heat then add the oil. Add the shallots and garlic followed by the sambal belacan shortly after. Mix through for 30 seconds then add the kangkung.

Add the soy sauce and 2 tablespoons water. Toss then cover the wok with a domed lid for 30 seconds, allowing the vegetable to cook through. Remove the lid and toss once again before removing from the heat and serving.

INDEX

ACKNOWLEDGEMENTS

Thanks to my mum and dad, Molly and Joe for providing us with the best quality produce and nourishing food while we were growing up. My mum in particular, for showing me ways to prepare and cook ingredients with utmost respect.

My sister Pam, who helped me with the sourcing of ingredients, prepping and cooking all 88 recipes for this book. I could not have done it without someone who understands my style of cooking and authenticity of flavours.

Gemma Smith and Yvonne Huang for the extra set of hands in the studio, prepping, cooking and cleaning.

Lee Blaylock for your incredible skills in bringing food to life through styling and passion.

Armelle Habib for your amazing set of eyes. You create magic through the lenses that no one else can and thank you for your studio. It was the perfect space for the book.

My good mate Lefty Arhon from Tim and Terry Oyster Supplies for supplying me with the freshest and highest quality seafood for the whole book.

Simon Davis, Antonietta Anello and the rest of the team at Hardie Grant who worked tirelessly to bring this book to life. It has been a great pleasure working with each and everyone in the team to create a masterpiece.

My dear friend Rushani Epa, thank you for believing and trusting in me and more importantly, convincing me to write a book in the first place. There wouldn't be *The Golden Wok* if not for you.

ABOUT THE AUTHOR

Born in Malaysia, Diana moved to Australia at the age of 18, and was blown away by the fresh produce available. Quickly finding her feet in the kitchen, the self-taught chef won the ninth season of *MasterChef Australia* in 2017 and has gone on to make a name for herself as a menu designer, product creator, restaurateur, content creator and host of SBS's *Asia Unplated* and Channel 10's *Ten Minute Kitchen*. She has a range of dumplings under the brand Golden Wok in all major supermarkets across Australia and looking to expand into Asia in 2025. She currently splits her time between Singapore and Melbourne.

Published in 2024 by Hardie Grant Books, an imprint of Hardie Grant Publishing

Hardie Grant Books (Melbourne)
Wurundjeri Country
Building 1, 658 Church Street
Richmond, Victoria 3121

Hardie Grant North America
2912 Telegraph Ave
Berkeley, California 94705

hardiegrant.com/books

Hardie Grant acknowledges the Traditional Owners of the Country on which we work, the Wurundjeri People of the Kulin Nation and the Gadigal People of the Eora Nation, and recognises their continuing connection to the land, waters and culture. We pay our respects to their Elders past and present.

NATIONAL LIBRARY OF AUSTRALIA

A catalogue record for this book is available from the National Library of Australia

The Golden Wok: Master the art of wok cooking
ISBN 978 1 74379 969 7

10 9 8 7 6 5 4 3 2 1

Publisher: Simon Davis
Commissioning Editor: Rushani Epa
Head of Editorial: Jasmin Chua
Project Editor: Antonietta Anello
Editor: Alex McDivitt
Designer: George Saad Studio
Photographer: Armelle Habib
Stylist: Lee Blaylock
Design Manager: Kristin Thomas
Head of Production: Todd Rechner
Production Controller: Jessica Harvie

Colour reproduction by Splitting Image Colour Studio

Printed in China by Leo Paper Products LTD.